NUMBER FOURTEEN

The Walter Prescott Webb Memorial Lectures

Essays on Frontiers in
World History

[THE WALTER PRESCOTT WEBB MEMORIAL LECTURES]

Essays on Frontiers in World History

BY PHILIP WAYNE POWELL, W. J. ECCLES,
WARREN DEAN, LEONARD THOMPSON,
ROBIN W. WINKS

Edited with an Introduction by
GEORGE WOLFSKILL *and*
STANLEY PALMER

Published for the University of Texas at Arlington by
Texas A&M University Press: College Station

Library of Congress Cataloging in Publication Data
Main entry under title:

Essays on frontiers in world history.

(The Walter Prescott Webb memorial lectures ; 14)
Bibliography: p.
1. Frontier and pioneer life—Addresses, essays,
lectures. 2. Frontier thesis—Addresses, essays,
lectures. 3. History, Modern—Addresses, essays,
lectures. I. Powell, Philip Wayne. II. Wolfskill,
George, 1921–   . III. Palmer, Stanley H.
IV. University of Texas at Arlington. V. Series.
D210.E84 1983   909.08   83-45100
ISBN 0-89096-167-0

Printed in the United States of America
FIRST EDITION

Contents

Preface   vii

Introduction   3
    George Wolfskill and Stanley Palmer

North America's First Frontier, 1546–1603   12
    Philip Wayne Powell

The Frontiers of New France   42
    W. J. Eccles

Ecological and Economic Relationships in Frontier History:
São Paulo, Brazil   71
    Warren Dean

The Southern African Frontier in Comparative Perspective   101
    Leonard Thompson

Australia, the Frontier, and the Tyranny of Distance   135
    Robin W. Winks

MAPS   *facing page*

The Gran Chichimeca in the Sixteenth Century   12

The North Mexican Silver Frontier in the Sixteenth Century   18

Eighteenth-Century Canada and Its Dependencies   44

State of São Paulo, Brazil: Paulista West in the Eighteenth Century   72

Southern Africa in the Nineteenth Century   106

Australia in the Twentieth Century   138

Preface

A few years ago, on April 5, 1979, the History Department of the University of Texas at Arlington was host for the fourteenth annual Walter Prescott Webb Memorial Lectures. Those several hundred guests who attended heard stimulating lectures on comparative world frontiers. Walter Prescott Webb would no doubt have enjoyed this particular series of lectures because the frontier theme was dominant in most of his own work; indeed, the Webb frontier thesis, as well as that of Frederick Jackson Turner, received considerable attention and reexamination in the lectures.

Four of the essays in this volume represent lectures delivered by Professor Warren Dean of New York University, Professor W. J. Eccles of the University of Toronto, Professor Leonard Thompson of Yale University, and Professor Robin W. Winks, also of Yale University. The fifth essay, by Professor Philip Wayne Powell of the University of California at Santa Barbara, is the 1979 winner of the fifth annual Webb-Smith Essay Prize.

In the preparation of this volume the editors have incurred obligations along the way. We wish to express our gratitude to Rosario Garza and Tad Howington of the University of Texas at Arlington Library, Eleanor Forfang, Media Services Center, and Grover Grubb, chairman, Engineering Graphics, for their efforts with the maps, and to Earleen Cook, also of the library staff, for help with the complexities of the footnoting.

Finally, as always, we would like to thank Mr. C. B. Smith, Sr., of Austin, Texas. Mr. Smith, a student and longtime friend of Professor Webb, has shown continuing interest in the Webb Lectures and has been generous in his financial support, which has included the establishment of the Webb-Smith Essay Prize. The Department of History and the University of Texas at Arlington are pleased to acknowledge the aid of this benefactor.

GEORGE WOLFSKILL
STANLEY PALMER

Essays on Frontiers in
World History

GEORGE WOLFSKILL and STANLEY PALMER

Introduction

ASK Americans—those from the United States, anyway—what they think of when they hear the word *frontier*. The answer is almost certain to be something about cowboys and Indians, longhorns and buffaloes, and shoot-outs on Main Street.

Ask most American historians—again those from the United States—what they think of when they hear the word *frontier*. The answer is almost certain to include the names of those historians most associated with frontier history, Frederick Jackson Turner and Walter Prescott Webb.

Yet neither Turner nor Webb thought of themselves in such restricted terms. Turner, in "The Significance of the Frontier in American History," his most famous work, was probably less concerned with the frontier as a phenomenon than he was with identifying a recurring theme around which to organize and synthesize a national history of the United States. The frontier was important to the extent that it gave meaning to a much larger story.

Walter Prescott Webb, although an offspring of the sand and sun, the ceaseless wind, and the bone-chilling cold of West Texas, did not consider himself a "frontier," or even a "Western," historian. In his most celebrated work, *The Great Plains*, which received the Loubat Prize of Columbia University, Webb was less concerned with the frontier concept than he was with demonstrating that the West, the trans-Mississippi West, was not like the East. The West had developed its own style, its own institutions, its own culture, not because it was a frontier, but because of its differing physical circumstances.

In his last important work, *The Great Frontier*, Webb conceived of the New World discoveries as the Great Frontier for England and Western Europe—the Metropolis, he called them. But Webb's Great Frontier/Metropolis concept dealt less with the nature of that frontier than with the economic boom in European civilization that the frontier created.

If Turner and Webb were not frontier historians in the strictest sense, they nevertheless triggered a healthy and enthusiastic interest in the study of the frontier phenomenon. That interest eventually carried beyond merely the study of a frontier to comparative studies of frontiers, in which the stated objective more often than not was to put the Turner/Webb theses to the test.

The definition of *frontier* was implicit in many if not most of these early comparative studies. The frontier was thought of as a land mass of varying size, a belt of land perhaps beyond the settled parts, where newcomers sought to appropriate land and its resources, usually at the expense of aborigines.

But the definition was not to remain that simple. It had not been that simple with Turner or Webb. There was a time when Turner was content to define frontier simply as the "thin red line," the "barometric line that recorded the advance of settlement," a line that separated the settled from the unsettled, the "meeting point between savagery and civilization."[1] The definition, however, gave way to the idea that the frontier was not just a line or even an area, but rather a complex process, always in a state of becoming.

The process included the steady spread of settlement, the economic, political, and social changes in the lands at the edge of settlement, the recurring settlement of successive areas of land, and the evolution of these successive areas from primitive pioneer life to what Turner considered the final state, that of an urban manufacturing society. "As you know," Turner wrote to a friend, "the 'West' with which I dealt, was a process rather than a fixed geographical region. . . ."[2] Turner thought of these successive areas, each in a different stage of development, as colonies of the eastern United States, and an understanding of "the interior," as he called these areas, was "a necessary element in an understanding of the America of the time." And in addition to all else, Turner was well aware that the frontier was, as much as anything, a state of mind.

As Webb used the term in *The Great Plains*, the frontier was a line that marked "the stark contrast between the East and the West." In his definition the ninety-eighth meridian was the frontier, "a sort of institutional fault line separating two physical environments, two animal kingdoms, two vegetable kingdoms and, finally, two human cultures, ancient and modern, i.e., Indian and European."[3]

But Webb had some of the same problems defining the frontier that Turner did. If the frontier was a line in *The Great Plains*, it became space and process in *The Great Frontier*. Not only that. The way Webb used newfound continents as "frontiers" for Europe at least implied that Turner's recurring frontiers within North America did not really matter much.

Webb's definition emerged from a series of questions. "What effect," he asked, "did the uncovering of three new continents around 1500 have on the civilization that discovered and for a time owned the continents? How did the sudden acquisition of all that land affect the individual," Webb wanted to know, "and the institutions of the time such as absolutism, democracy, slavery, and religious policy."[4]

But the key question was what all that land (frontier) did to economic practice (process). The answer was that the New World discoveries, what Webb called the Great Frontier, precipitated a boom for the European Metropolis. According to his hypothesis, it was the boom which produced new institutions such as capitalism, participatory democracy, and the modern concept of progress. The "big boom, based on all the resources of the Great Frontier," Webb wrote somewhat pessimistically, "lasted so long that it was considered normal and its institutions permanent."[5]

Those who have since taken up the work of studying the frontier phenomenon and of comparing frontiers have not only challenged the "line and process" concepts of Turner and Webb, but they have also gone beyond, asking new questions and framing new definitions. The basic questions, of course, still remain: What is a frontier? Are there different types of frontiers? How long does a frontier stay a frontier? Or is there no time limit?

These and other related questions have sometimes produced provocative results. The frontier may, for example, have had to do with the way aborigines were viewed, which provided approval for behavior that might otherwise be considered immoral or illegal at the very least. The treatment of the American Indian, of course, instantly comes to mind.

The questioning and testing of the Turner/Webb definitions have led to a rather wide variety of demographic models and classification systems for studying and comparing frontiers. The authors in this volume of the Webb Memorial Lectures series are among those who have made notable contributions to that historiography of comparative frontiers. Their essays are arranged in approximate chronological order based on the most critical frontier period with which each is concerned. The volume commences with Philip Wayne Powell's essay, winner of the Webb-Smith Essay Prize, on the Gran Chichimeca. That work is followed by W. J. Eccles's essay on New France. The histories of both regions are closely related to the frontier history of the United States. The scene then shifts to Brazil, still in the Western Hemisphere but approached by Warren Dean somewhat differently than Powell or Eccles approached their areas. These areas are in contrast to two frontier segments of the British Empire—South Africa, the subject of Leonard Thompson's essay, and Australia, the subject of Robin Winks's essay. The five essays are truly wide-ranging, spanning four continents and a time frame of some four hundred years.

The authors have produced provocative essays with contrasting emphases and differing conclusions. In inviting them to contribute to this volume, we asked all of them to employ essentially the same formula, that of discussing the physical environment and aborigines, the incursion of a new culture, and the interaction of that new culture with the indigenous one. They acknowledge their debt to Turner and Webb and, in the case of Powell, to another great historian of the American frontier, Herbert Eugene Bolton, and they relate their essays to the existing body of literature for their respective frontiers.

Powell emphasizes the fact that the presence of a precious resource was the prime consideration on the northern Mexican frontier. The plateau between the eastern and the western Sierras Madres north of Mexico City contained fabulous wealth—the Silver Frontier of the Gran Chichimeca. In order to protect the borderlands silver mines, roads, missions, towns, and stock-raising haciendas, the Spanish government pursued primarily defensive military policies and, finally, an aggressive diplomacy among the Chichimeca Nations. These policies were refined and used repeatedly on later frontiers. Once pacified, the Gran Chichimeca of New Spain became a base for further penetration into New Mexico and then Texas.

The theme of violent warfare and enslavement of the conquered Chichimecas dominates the period of initial contact with the aborigines. But it, in turn, was followed by a policy of pacification which was remarkably successful and developed some quite positive features in racial relations: such things as the concept of amnesty, the providing of sustenance during transitional or "civilizing" periods, training in husbandry, and religious accommodation.

Powell is quite sensitive to the remarkable similarities in the physical environment of the Gran Chichimeca and the land that Webb wrote about—similarities that produced adaptations in such things as transport, technology, commercial activity, and labor utilization. The similarities carried over into matters that would be more familiar to lay persons—especially moviegoers—for example, Indian attacks on trains of covered wagons, widespread use of horse and gun, stock rustling, Chichimeca ways of torturing captives, employment of friendly Indians as military allies and scouts, preference of primitive Indian Chiefs for dealing with military officers rather than the clergy in making peace, and the importance of presidios.

In the second essay, Eccles asserts unequivocally that the Turner thesis does not fit the circumstances encountered in New France. There was no frontier "line"; instead, there was a series of lines of great length and no breadth along the water routes, fanning out to the north, south, and west. Unlike the Anglo American and the Spanish experience, this frontier was not one of settlement. New France was a river empire.

If the Gran Chichimeca was a silver frontier, New France was a fur frontier. In exploiting the fur trade, the French developed a special relationship with the aborigines. The French, Eccles argues, were never numerous enough to threaten the native peoples. Moreover, in their struggles with the British, the French were dependent on the Indians for help. They therefore tried not to offend the Indians. Unlike natives in other places who were conquered and sometimes enslaved by newcomers, the Indians of New France remained free, retained sovereignty over their lands, and, in fact, only tolerated the isolated French trading posts because there they obtained the European goods they wanted.

In the continuing debate over the persistence of change of institutions on the frontier, Eccles asserts that few original or enduring institutions resulted from the development of New France. Traces of democracy were minimal. Institutions at the parish level mirrored those in the mother country. On the frontier of New France, historical change tended to result not from local circumstances but from events and decisions made in Europe. "The long arm of the government at Versailles," Eccles notes, "reached far out into the wilderness."

The frontiers of South America that have received any serious attention have almost invariably been those identified with an important crop readily lending itself to world commerce. The Paulista West, a huge area and a frontier of sugar and coffee in the interior of the Brazilian state of São Paulo, is no exception. Dean's essay concentrates on the ecological impact of human occupation and of sugar and coffee cultivation on that environment. Other themes, such as the treatment of the aborigines, the role of government, and institutional change, are subordinated and are important only as they contribute to an understanding of the major theme, the ecological degradation of the environment.

Of the factors contributing to that degradation, the most serious was speculative capitalist agriculture largely responsible for the system called *swidden* or *slash-and-burn*. This system is one widely used in the tropical forests of Southeast Asia and Africa as well as South America. In simplest terms it consists of cutting the trees and underbrush on an area selected for cultivation, leaving the cuttings to dry, and, before the start of the rainy season, burning off the area. The resulting ash acts as a natural fertilizer, making the soil unusually rich, but only for a brief time—perhaps three to five years. The land is then abandoned, sometimes for as long as twenty to twenty-five years. The process is then repeated.

The exploitative nature of sugar and coffee horticulture, stockraising, and later gold and silver mining (in Minas Gerais, Mato Grosso, and Goiás) not only transformed the economy of the Paulista West but also radically altered its racial composition. Military companies known as *bandeiras* enslaved or eradicated tribes as far as the Paraná River. The shifting cultivation of sugar and coffee attracted an exotic mixture of blacks, mestizos, Spaniards, Italians, and even a few Japanese, along with the Portuguese. The result was a cultural pluralism not reflected in the older areas.

In Southern Africa, unusual geographic and environmental factors allowed a very small group of settlers at the Cape of Good Hope to occupy a territory the size of Great Britain before being challenged by the powerful Bantu-speaking farmers. That eventual encounter aggravated racist tendencies that were already present in the southwestern part of the colony—tendencies that became strong and persistent in subsequent relations between Afrikaners and the native Africans.

As settlers moved north and east, farther and farther away from the arable southwest, they had little choice but to become stock farmers, some families running sheep and cattle on areas of six thousand acres or more. This practice helped to produce a unified culture reinforced by the fact that the good harbors and an outlet to the world economy were concentrated in the Cape area—meaning that all political, economic, and cultural institutions emanated from the Cape. The patriarchal family became the standard social unit, and the men formed *commandos* (a word of Dutch-Afrikaans origin) to acquire mastery over the aboriginal hunters.

Thompson shows that attempts at central control of the frontier from the Cape were weak and halfhearted in both the Dutch and British systems. The British did not make serious efforts to prevent some of the stock farmers from leaving the Cape Colony for the interior, where they maintained their traditional mode of life, while the British administration modified the institutions in the Cape Colony. These migrants later became known as *Voortrekkers*, and their migration as the *Great Trek*—the central saga in Afrikaner nationalist historiography.

Winks's essay on Australia places considerable emphasis on the attitude toward aborigines by contrasting Australia with New Zealand. Immigrants to Australia were often convicts transported half a world away from home. Many were illiterate and brutalized, with little or no appreciation of human worth. The aborigines—dark and physically unattractive by British standards—seemed to stimulate among the immigrants racial prejudice that contributed finally to a policy of annihilation.

But newcomers to New Zealand, as Winks points out, came of their own accord, seeking to re-create the best of that which British society denied them at home. The aborigines, the Maoris, were judged by the settlers to be a relatively attractive people with a complex indigenous society, settled villages, and a highly developed religion. Here the policy was one of assimilation. By the end of the nineteenth century the Maoris were given full citizenship and representation in government. Winks states that the native policy in Australia was in some ways similar to that in the United States, while the New Zealand policy was more akin to the accommodationist approach in Canada.

There is, of course, a great deal more in these essays than has thus far been indicated. The reader will learn, in passing, something of the significance in frontier development of missions, missionaries, religion, presidios, soldiers, wars, slavery, reservations, race, disease, gold, silver, diamonds, transportation, government, and many other factors.

The essays are independent of each other; from essay to essay there is no explicit comparative dialogue. Moreover, they are straightforward, what might be called "traditional" history; each writer looks for institutional development in the frontier of his choice. In fulfilling their assignments—providing an overview of their current research on the frontiers—the authors of these essays have done their work and done it well.

If the essays stand alone, they are nonetheless interrelated. It is eminently clear, for example, that each writer is, in his own way, attempting to move away from the Turner-Webb line-and-process concept of the frontier to one that emphasizes the frontier, so neatly defined by Thompson, as "an area of interpenetration between societies." And the essays share a certain melancholic mood, a pessimism resulting from the consensus that, regardless of time or place, these frontiers have closed and that this closing was not for the better. In that sense, each author deserves the label, to use Winks's own term, of "catastrophic" historian.

Walter Webb once conceded, with his sly, crooked grin, that

he preferred "the frontier theory over the frontier in fact."[6] Webb would be pleased with the frontier in theory as well as the frontier in fact of these stimulating essays.

NOTES

1. Quoted in Wilbur R. Jacobs, John W. Caughey, and Joe B. Frantz, *Turner, Bolton, and Webb* (Seattle: University of Washington Press, 1965), pp. 8, 13.

2. Ibid.

3. Ibid., pp. 83–84.

4. Ibid., p. 88.

5. Ibid., p. 89.

6. Ibid., p. 95.

PHILIP WAYNE POWELL

North America's First Frontier, 1546–1603

IN long perspective and in the sense created by Anglo-American experience, this continent's first frontier was an upcountry advance of settlement and civilization set in motion by the 1546–48 discoveries of silver in Mexico's Zacatecas Sierras. The sequent rush of Forty-Eighters and Forty-Niners, pioneer opportunity seekers and adventurous home builders, began Mexico's "Silver Age," with global reverberations, imperial and commercial. The opening of this mother lode also began three centuries and more of European-guided thrust into the heartland of the northern New World.

Almost overnight, this first frontier became a melting pot of disparate racial and cultural elements and levels—American Indian, European, and African—that quickened formation of a Mexican people and was the first phase of a northward flow of "Mexican" blood that reaches our times. This frontier was the cornerstone of later Spanish-Mexican colonization and empire building, genesis of a basic ingredient of North American history. Failure to recognize and understand this first frontier inhibits any genuine search for identity by those of Mexican lineage who, by northward marches— theirs or ancestral—are now United States westerners.

Terminologically, this first of the Spanish Borderlands can rightfully be called the "Silver Frontier" or, better, the "Chichimeca Frontier," thus commemorating the aboriginal inhabitants and fitting sixteenth-century usage. Chronologically, it began in 1546 and closed, or "passed beyond," at century's turning, when the farther Nueva Vizcaya and more distant New Mexico became the new frontiers. The dozen years after 1590 embraced a pacification process that ended the bloody and terribly destructive forty-year conflict called the Chichimeca War (1550–90), first and longest of North America's military showdowns between a sophisticated society— the northward-moving, clothes-wearing Indians, Spaniards, Ne-

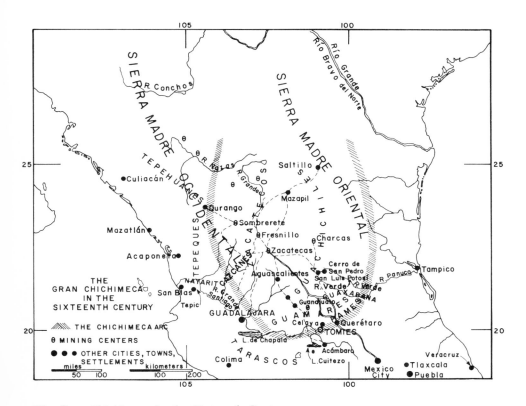

The Gran Chichimeca in the Sixteenth Century

groes, and mixtures of these—and a very primitive people, the very
naked Chichimeca Nations. A massive official investigation of this
Chichimeca Peace was completed in 1603, an event that serves better than most to close this frontier story.

Geographically, this Gran Chichimeca was largely limited to
the plateau lying between the two great Sierras Madres, east and
west. Its southern edge was a curve hinged on the west just north
of Guadalajara, and, on the east, in Querétaro country, dipping to
the twentieth parallel east of Lake Chapala. There was no northern
limit except the vast unknown beyond the Chichimeca Nations, horizons that did not begin to acquire civilization's nomenclature until
the closing years of the first frontier's life. In effect, however, and
within the definable sixteenth-century story, the northern edge was
the farthest reaches of those called the Chichimecas: roughly, an
east-west line between the towns of Saltillo and Durango.

Since this early Mexican frontier is so little known, I preface
my delineation of its people and institutions with a brief historical
summary and some parallels and contrasts with the later, more familiar Anglo-American experiences. This unorthodox introduction
may help to bridge the cultural and chronological chasm between
the very recent and the distant; between the very Anglo and the
quintessentially Ibero-American.[1]

The Zacatecas strike triggered a quick opening of north-south
roads, binding that wilderness bonanza to the lands of Cortesian
Conquest. Three routes in the west linked the new mother lode to
Guadalajara country, whence came the discoverers and earliest
miners. Far more important was the Mexico City–Zacatecas road,
some 350 miles of Royal Inland Highway (*Camino Real de la Tierra
Adentro*), overnight creation of the Silver Rush. This principal road
fastened the new frontier to the civilized south, thence to the vital
Mexico-Veracruz artery and transatlantic shipping. Immediate heavy
demands upon this Silver Highway impelled quick improvement to
accommodate the largest wagons, two-axled *carros*, in addition to
the customary pack trains and two-wheeled *carretas*. This was the
continent's first great wilderness road and first stretch of a fifteen-
hundred-mile wagon road that, near century's turn, began feeding
the colonization of New Mexico.

Travelers and cargo on the new roads immediately quickened

the marauding talents of the Chichimeca warriors, who now constituted a far-spread ambush of the strangers crossing their ancestral
hunting, warring, and trading paths. Chichimeca braves began
plundering this traffic in 1550, thereby opening a forty-year war of
death and destruction that paled memory of the Cortés-Aztec clash.
The costs of this Chichimeca War—in time, property, and lives—
far exceeded those of Cortés's invasion, and this seemingly endless
collision of Naked Ones and Clothes-Wearers was the major human
drama of this early frontier.[2]

During four decades after mid-century, the Chichimeca War
was an agonizing experience for Europeans and for the sedentary,
sophisticated Indians who were the bulk of the northward advance.
The incoming southerners never completely adapted themselves to
the hit-and-run, ambush style of guerrilla fighting waged by the
wilderness warriors. The newcomers did not even become truly
accustomed to their tormenters' nudity, a continuing shock, especially for the European mind.

The Chichimeca bowman, in his own territory and contiguous
lands, was so formidable a fighter that he was never overcome in
war by the European and Indian intruders. And the northern brave
grew more redoubtable in the last decade of the war, when his
attacks became more effective with use of the horse. The Chichimeca Peace of the 1590s was purchased through diplomacy and gift-
giving; it was not a military triumph for the Clothes-Wearers. This
first failure of sedentary peoples to cope with the warfare of primitive nomadic and seminomadic New World Indians was echoed in
later continental history.

The awesome prowess of the wilderness warrior, on his own
ground, makes understandable the pervasive preoccupation of the
new frontier people with defense against Chichimeca attack. It also
made this frontier something quite distinct from so-called Spanish
Conquest. As we shall see, the Chichimeca War reversed the Conquest pattern of individualistic and "joint-stock company" initiatives—devoid of, and antagonistic to, governmental participa-
tion—and stirred the borderland settlers to clamor for Crown support
and supervision of their defense.

Because of the intruders' slow adjustment to Chichimeca tactics, the northern war intensified during the first two decades. At

one point, 1561, populous Zacatecas was in a virtual state of siege, isolated by Chichimeca attacks. Even so, the great veins of the Guanajuato Sierras were found, and work was begun there in the middle 1550s; outlying ranches were raided, but the main mining center, growing rapidly, was not seriously threatened. However, other discoveries, far from population strength (for example, Mazapil, Sombrerete, Chalchihuites, San Martín, Charcas), lived precariously, suffered much difficulty in receiving supplies and sending out silver, and were sometimes abandoned.

New Spain's fourth viceroy, Martín Enríquez (1568–80), was the first to make the Chichimeca War a primary subject of governmental attention. Responding to the frontier people's clamor, and to the demonstrated weaknesses of private defense, Enríquez quickly introduced the presidio on the northern frontier, first as defense for the Mexico-Zacatecas Road, then for protection of other travel routes and strategic locations. Simultaneously, the viceroy strengthened and more closely supervised the northern military stance by appointing able men, usually university-educated judges, to the posts of *teniente de capitán general* in the Mexican and Guadalajara audiencias, thus beginning a long history of such high-ranking leadership for the borderlands. Don Martín also initiated special taxation to support frontier soldiery and presidios. From his time to the end of Spanish rule there was always a category of "Gastos de Guerra" in the royal treasury; it was temporarily called "Gastos de la Paz" when the Chichimeca conflict was winding down in the 1590s.

Of major importance, the Enríquez administration inaugurated and presided over the beginnings of debate—by high clergy, other officials, and men experienced in the northern war—on the controversial subject of the justice, or injustice, of waging war against the hostile aborigines, a juridicial-moral problem close to Crown conscience since the days of Queen Isabel and New World discovery. The majority, viewing the fight against the Chichimecas as justifiable defense, recommended a kind of total war, called *guerra a fuego y a sangre* ("war by fire and blood"), thereby making legal a limited enslavement for those captured and proven guilty of raiding. The main opponents of this decision were, as was to be expected, the Dominican brothers and heirs of Antonio de Montesinos and Bartolomé de las Casas.[3]

Enslavement of captured Chichimecas continued into the next decade, but such servitude was limited by the precedents set by Viceroy Enríquez. Clerical reversal of the "just" war decision, plus increasing attention to the evils of sales of the captured enemy by soldiers, brought leanings toward pacification in the 1580s. Meanwhile, the Chichimeca War continued and intensified, reaching a critical stage in the late seventies and early eighties.

These crisis years generated a royal decision toward greater liberality in financial support, a rapid increase of frontier soldiery, additional presidios to a total of more than fifty, and predictable complaint from the frontier people that all this was not enough. The years of heightened conflict coincided with some weakness in the viceregal government (the early death of Enríquez's successor, then interim governance by the Mexican Audiencia and the archbishop) along with clerical change to unanimity against the war and Chichimeca enslavement, expressed in the Third Mexican Synod in 1585.

At this historical moment a dynamic new viceroy, the Marqués de Villamanrique, came on the scene. A forceful and impatient governor, the Marqués quickly saw the Chichimeca War as the most important immediate problem of the realm and determined to end it by a drastic cut in frontier soldiery and presidios. He thus sought to halt the frontier slave traffic by removing its principal practitioners, hoping thereby to stop the war by eliminating a basic cause of Chichimeca hostility.

Such sudden reversal of policy threw a scare into the frontier people and caused grave concern among those most experienced in the Gran Chichimeca. More moderate views finally turned Villamanrique toward a safer and more promising end of war and of the Chichimeca enslavement he so strongly condemned.

During 1587–89, much under the influence of the frontier's only mestizo captain, Miguel Caldera (half Spanish and half Chichimeca), the Villamanrique administration fashioned a Chichimeca Peace based on gift-giving diplomacy; protection of those accepting peace and settlement against attack by Indians still hostile or against mistreatment by the Clothes-Wearers; continuing government rations of food, clothing, and utensils; and training in husbandry and in Christian religion and ways.

Responsibility for this peace program was soon inherited by

the able and widely respected Viceroy Luis de Velasco (1590–95), who had served as a frontier general. Don Luis wisely retained Captain Caldera, now titled "Chief Justice [Justicia Mayor], of all the new settlements," in immediate command of the pacification process. In doing so, Velasco described the wilderness-born mestizo as "the man most necessary in all these realms for making the Chichimeca Peace; the first and foremost promoter of this peace."[4] Viceroy the Conde de Monterrey (1595–1603) presided over completion of the peace, including the *visita* of 1601–1603, which describes, in detail, this innovative milestone in North America frontier history.

Throughout the Chichimeca War, mining—mainly of silver—grew in output and in technical refinement of smelting and amalgamation (patio) processes, especially in areas of sizable population (Zacatecas, Guanajuato), but it remained precarious and rudimentary in outlying, smaller settlements, with frequent reports of slowdown and abandonment because of Chichimeca attacks. The peace, in a near-symbolic demonstration of its benefits to the frontier people, triggered another major discovery, that of San Luis Potosí (Cerro de San Pedro), in 1592 by Captain Caldera, who was then supervising diplomacy and gift-giving among the Guachichiles, strongest and largest of the Chichimeca Nations.

While the pull of successive silver strikes projected settlement into distant, isolated, and dangerous places, separated from southern civilization by vast stretches of *despoblado* (uninhabited land; wilderness), the *tierra de guerra* of Chichimeca ambush, there was also a slower, more compact northward advance spilling over the southern edges of the "Chichimeca Arc." In this nearer borderland, stock raising, accompanied by some related town founding (for example, of Celaya, Apaseo), pushed outward from crowded conditions in the lands of Cortesian victory. Thus, Querétaro country and the Michoacán-Guanajuato border steadily filled with *estancias*, ranches producing not only cattle, horses, mules, and smaller stock but also homesites for *estancieros* and their retinues, including the hardy cowboy (*vaquero*), who often doubled as Chichimeca fighter. Stock raising was also, of course, a necessary adjunct of mining and was thus an extension of the mining camps and towns.

Characteristically, and sometimes by government requirement

in land grants, the borderland *estancias* not only provided fighting men for defense and reprisal in the Chichimeca War but also gave defensive shelter to travelers in what was called the *casafuerte* (literally, "strong house"), a kind of "minifort." And it was stock ranching that spearheaded the Clothes-Wearers' advance into the San Francisco Valley of southern Guachichil country, opening up the large region that came to be called San Luis Potosí.

Starting early in its life, the Silver Frontier's capital, manpower, and provisions gave basic support to farther borderlands. Thus, Francisco de Ibarra's early explorations into the northwestern sierras, a province that came to be called, with good Basque love of the motherland, Nueva Vizcaya, were supplied from Zacatecas country. This new province in the west, and Monterrey in the east, became, at century's end, the next frontiers.

Similarly, the sixteenth-century Gran Chichimeca made possible the advance to New Mexico. Without an understanding of the antecedent frontier, the New Mexico story is rootless. And the later advance into Texas was also based upon wealth, lands, stock, and families traceable to the first frontier. The Marqués de Aguayo, leading the Texas enterprise, was the heir of a vast mineral, ranching, and commercial estate begun by Captain Alonso López de Loys (Mazapil and Río Grande) and greatly expanded by his son-in-law, Captain Francisco de Urdiñola, a Basque who rose from common frontier soldier to become viceregal first choice to lead the New Mexico colonization. (This appointment was wrested from him because of a feuding rival's false charges that he had murdered his wife and some employees, but Urdiñola was acquitted and then served more than a decade as governor of the more valuable Nueva Vizcaya.)

This first frontier contained almost every element and episode of the kinds that later stretched to global fame out of Anglo-American expansion. Thus, the Mexico-Zacatecas Road (and others) was the scene of many a Chichimeca attack upon trains of covered wagons, and those who fell before such onslaughts were scalped, tortured, and carried into captivity, in the way of Anglo westerns and Hollywood epics. In the early decades, such Chichimeca raids were carried out by warriors on foot, much as forest Indians fought on early Anglo frontiers; later raids were by Indian horsemen, as in the trans-

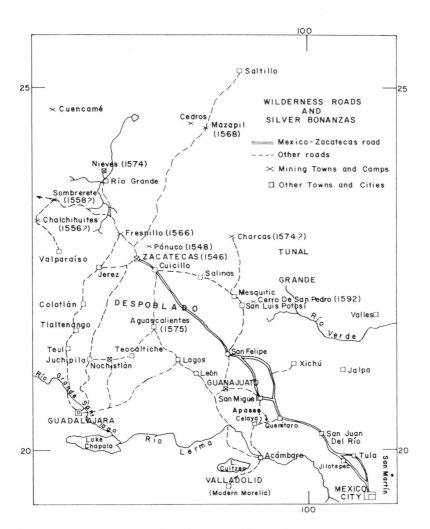

The North Mexican Silver Frontier in the Sixteenth Century

Mississippi West. Early fighting on the Chichimeca Frontier was a confrontation of sword and arquebus against bow and arrow, similar to the first eastern-seaboard fighting of whites and Indians and differing from the later combat that engaged rifles, six-shooters, and widespread Indian use of guns and horses. However, Chichimeca skill, speed, and penetrating power with bow and arrow—not excelled anywhere, according to awed chroniclers from Europe—must have approximated (or bettered?) the accuracy of Plains Indians' use of rifles on horseback.

As in later continental history, this early frontier was much affected by the slowness with which Europeans adapted to the warring ways of the Naked Ones. On the Chichimeca frontier, there were episodes that read like Braddock's Defeat and Custer's Last Stand; it was a frequent complaint that loss of life and property resulted from the appointment of some captains and generals inexperienced in frontier circumstances and ignorant or fatally disdainful of Chichimeca bravery and tactics. During the 1580s frontier warfare came more into the hands of experienced captains, such as Juan Morlete, Miguel Caldera, Francisco de Urdiñola, and the famous General Rodrigo del Río de Loza, who, in many years of war against Chichimecas, rose from common soldier to general.

In the manner of later North American history, the Chichimecas were romanticized and defended by distant men who did not know them as well as did the frontier people suffering from their raids and rustling. (We must be mindful that the "noble savage" was created by sixteenth-century Spaniards, and that Jean Jacques Rousseau was a latecomer to this vision.) Thus, it was easier for Dominicans than Franciscans to view the Chichimeca War as unjust and declaim against enslavement of the primitives; for the Black Friars, the distant Chichimeca was an abstraction, unknown at first hand. Franciscans, however, with an early roll of martyrs to Chichimeca arrows and torture, not only became reluctant to enter such service but also generally favored the policy of *guerra a fuego y a sangre*. These frontier friars, notably unsuccessful in attracting the Chichimeca until the captains and viceregal government structured peace in the nineties, were often antagonistic to any "soft" treatment of Chichimecas because of their attacks on the peaceful, Christianized Indians so beloved of the padres.

The debate on "just" war and affinitive Chichimeca enslave-ment took place, of course, in the viceregal capital and grew out of the "lascasian" leanings of royal conscience. Such a debate would have been unthinkable in the frontier environment, where the only "good" Chichimecas were either dead or enslaved; in this, of course, there is some parallelism with later Eastern Seaboard attitudes to-ward a distant, abstract Indian compared with the frontier people's close-up of the red man.

There are other parallels in types, attitudes, and dramatic epi-sodes: the stock-rustling ("horse-thievin'") hostile; captured white women among the Chichimecas (as also mestizos, mulattoes, Chris-tian Indians—and the ransoming and rescue thereof); pacified Chi-chimecas serving as scouts and allies against those still hostile; the warring chiefs' noticeable preference to deal diplomatically with their white military counterparts rather than with missionaries or others; the unpopularity of frontier military service against the Indian war-rior, with desertions and deaths accounting for rapid personnel turnover; fort, or presidio, systems and the defensive stockade, or *casafuerte*; the ubiquitous mule pack train accompanying military or diplomatic forays into hostile Indian country; the ritualistic powwows of Indian chiefs and white captains; and so on.

There are some notable contrasts, too, that contribute to an understanding of the first frontier by comparing it with later ones. Spanish-Mexican horsemanship and expert use of pack animals were surely superior to the Anglo versions, and, in fact, much of this earlier knowledge of livestock was transmitted to westward-moving Anglos, along with more than a little of the vocabulary pertaining thereto.

There was no truly professional military force on the Chichi-meca Frontier. The fighting was done mainly by frontier settlers (home builders, often heads of families, who were only temporar-ily—and not always—in royal pay) or adventurous opportunity seekers who usually became frontier residents. Surprise attacks on Indian villages, with extermination in mind, were not practiced by the Clothes-Wearers on the Chichimeca Frontier; the major objec-tive was the taking of captives for later sale or, beginning in the Enríquez administration, for placement in government hands for a limited servitude combined with training in civilized ways and Christianity.

Pacification efforts on the Chichimeca Frontier constituted a formal doctrine of Indian relations: amnesty; provisioning for sustenance during a transitional "civilizing" period; protection against other hostiles and Clothes-Wearers; training in husbandry; missionary attention; settlement on frontier lands (by contrast with the later Anglo practice of distant removal). All of this was aimed at early incorporation into a civilized society and its ways. This integrationist doctrine, sometimes attempted even during the earliest and bloodiest phases of the war, reached its highest success in the peace of the 1590s and became a basic part of Spanish-Mexican frontier policy and practice during the next two centuries and more. Such consistency of policy in borderland circumstances limns "Spain's frontiering genius" and is a striking contrast with the more random course of Indian policy in Anglo-America.[5]

These few examples in parallelism and contraposition will serve, I trust, to illuminate the distant "first" frontier. The more fundamental and significant characteristics of the earlier frontier—those elements most essential to historical reconstruction of it—are to be found, of course, in the makeup of the frontier people and their institutions—how they began, how they changed, and their interaction with environment.

The Frontier People

The aboriginal inhabitants of the Gran Chichimeca were classified by contemporary writers into nations (primarily Guachichiles, Zacatecos, Guamares, and Pames, with some subdivisions), and they were described as living in rancherías, or clusters of rancherías suggesting tribal relationship. Throughout the Gran Chichimeca life varied little, and it is thus conveniently valid to portray these peoples in general terms. There was greater homogeneity among the Chichimeca Nations than among the more complex and disparate "history-makers" who invaded their territory. Generalizations are thus more valid in the first case; fuller treatment and some basic distinctions are necessary in delineating the second.

In all the Gran Chichimeca, complete or near nudity was universal; women sometimes wore loin covers, like tiny skirts, and some men used a kind of breechclout which they discarded, when going into battle, "for the effect." Shelter was crude, usually a conical hut of thatch or a cave. Food was obtained by hunting and gathering; major components were rodents, snakes, frogs, birds, fish, deer, mesquite pods, acorns, roots and seeds, and cactus apples (*tunas*). Religious practices were primitive, hardly discernible to the more sophisticated invaders from the south. Chieftainship, locally limited and of low visibility, was so lacking in authority that it was a constant frustration to the Clothes-Wearers' diplomatic efforts.

During the four decades after 1550, natives of the Gran Chichimeca changed in significant ways. They became addicted to certain of the invaders' goods and customs, such as the meat of domesticated animals (mule meat became a great favorite) and other foods and the use of cloth and clothing, usually captured. As a result of enslavement or childhood training among the Clothes-Wearers, an increasing number of *ladinos* (those knowing the invaders' tongues and ways) came into being and, by their superior knowledge of the enemy, achieved strong chieftainship among the nations, thus making diplomatic relations more feasible and effective.

In areas of closest contact with sedentary peoples, diseases undoubtedly aggravated the attrition that came from war and capture. Although the Chichimecas were still raiding successfully in the eighties—often increasingly so, with horses and astute *ladino* leadership—such attrition, abetted by increasing desire for civilization's utensils and a more stable supply of food and clothing, certainly undermined the earlier intransigence of Chichimeca hostility and thus smoothed the way toward pacification.

By contrast with these native inhabitants of the Gran Chichimeca, the peoples moving into the area after 1546 were far more heterogeneous in blood, customs, migrational motives, and ancestral memories. To overcome the stylistic difficulty posed by the many and fundamental dissimilarities, while yet exploiting the universality of their sedentary ways, comparative sophistication, and use of body covering, I call them the "Clothes-Wearers," by contrast with the "Naked Ones."

The northward migration of the Clothes-Wearers took place under Spanish sovereignty, but it was, in the main, a non-Spanish movement. (Chroniclers of that time and later constantly refer to "Spaniards" by contrast with Chichimecas, but this must be understood as "the Spanish side," including Indians, Negroes, and mixtures.) Advance of settlement into this frontier was usually—but not always—guided by the Spanish-blooded minority, who provided mineral and town-founding initiatives and government for the greater numbers of Indians (such as Tarascans, Otomíes, Mexicas or Aztecs, Tlaxcalans, and Cholulans), free and slave Negroes and mulattoes, and all the mixtures of these elements.

This large migration was not of military makeup, nor was it a diplomatic-military thrust for sovereignty, as was the Cortesian Conquest. It was simply a move to new homes, a migration of settlers of the kind that so often occurred later in the continent. This Spanish-Indian-Negro expansion was, above all, not a part of so-called Spanish Conquest, which, in any case, was a collaborative Spanish-Indian overthrow of Aztec hegemony.

Spaniards going to the new frontier were themselves quite varied in class, origin, customs, and motives. There were mining men already moneyed by previous discoveries or other rewarding activity. There were the penniless, or nearly so, looking for adventure, with end-of-the-rainbow visions. There were government officials dedicated to royal service in the imperial bureaucracy and, likely enough, on the lookout for extra-official enrichment; churchmen, regular and secular, of all ranks (except bishop and archbishop); laborers of all kinds, either salaried or as relatives and retinue of the more affluent; artisans; businessmen, local or itinerant (for example, wagoner-merchants); salaried soldiery after 1568; charcoal makers and sellers; blacksmiths; innkeepers (men and women); and wives and children. One of the most notable elements was the sizable number of Basques, from blacksmiths to bonanza kings, who impressed their own and their *madre patria's* names upon the land and its history. There was also, in the white population, a sprinkling of other Europeans: Portuguese (many of them Jewish, or "New Christians"), Greek, English, French, Italian, Flemish, and German or Austrian.

The northward-moving Indians were, usually, laborers seeking

salaries, or retinue for entrepeneurial Spaniards and Indian governors and *principales*; defensive colonists, attracted by grants of
privileges (such as tax or tribute exemption) and lands given by the
viceregal government; military allies of Spanish-mestizo soldiery in
defensive or reprisal actions; some miners (for example, Otomíes in
San Luis Potosí country); many merchants (a popular occupation
among the advanced nations of the south and carried over into the
new frontier); and women and children as families of these pioneers.

Many of the frontier folk were mestizos, part of that rapidly
growing amalgam of Spaniard and Indian. In motive, occupation,
and social category they ranged all the way from the lowest vaga-
bonds to the affluent elite, such as the descendants of the Zacatecas
discoverer Juan de Tolosa, whose wife was the daughter of Hernán
Cortés and Doña Isabel Moctezuma. Within this wide range was
that heroic Spanish-Chichimeca mestizo of humble beginnings,
Captain and Frontier Justice Miguel Caldera, the first important
historical personage born in the North American wilderness. Most
mestizos among the frontier people were simple adventurers and
laborers engaged in the many varieties of mining and ranching labor or as local shopkeepers, artisans, or whatnot.

It will never be possible, of course, to ascertain how many Negroes and mulattoes, slave and free, migrated to this frontier, but
they were a goodly percentage of the Clothes-Wearers' total. They
were early taken as slaves for mining, and this practice continued
through the century and beyond. Free Negroes and mulattoes, who
were a noticeably large population segment in New Spain by the
seventies, engaged themselves for salaries or as retinue in most
every laboring category; thus, among other things, they served as
public criers and as vaqueros. And during the entire life of this
frontier, *cimarrones*, escaped Negro slaves, raided travel routes and
outlying settlements, sometimes in alliance with Chichimeca braves.
There were also *zambos* (of Indian-Negro mixture), of course, and
most other imaginable kinds and percentages of mixture, making
the people of the Chichimeca Frontier as colorful as any in the New
World in deed, culture, and complexion.

The frontier people inevitably changed in the contradistinctive circumstances of this strange wilderness zone. Peculiarities of northern mining; the broader, freer horizons of stock raising; the burdens of greater travel distances between settlements; the constant Chichimeca danger; the unfamiliarity of large stretches of aridity; differing flora and fauna—all these factors and more went into the reshaping of these first northerners into a frontier breed new in the Mexican land.

The earliest mining camps, virtually without governmental authority in their first months of existence, were scenes of fighting, feuding, claim jumping, and all the turbulence made famous on later frontiers. Even with officialdom's arrival, the northern mining towns were noted for law evasion, fraud in tax matters, and stealing in mines and ore-processing areas. It was a need for audit of the royal treasury office (*real caja*) in Zacatecas that produced the large 1601–1603 Visita of the Chichimeca Peace. This was a land where fighting weapons, ceaseless litigation, and frequency of jail use were close companions of the silver flow. From those days to these, the Mexican *norteño* has been a conspicuous carrier of weapons. Traditional intimacy with arms, combined with notable hardiness in horsemanship born of distances and toughness of terrain, forged a Northerner who, in our times, was a commanding force in the 1910 Revolution. The prototype of this famous cavalry was born on the Chichimeca Frontier.

The wider horizons and sparse aboriginal population, almost imperceptibly based in mountain lairs, made of this frontier's stock raising the vast haciendas that still characterize the region and a way of life far more expansive than was possible or legal in most lands of the Cortesian Conquest. Even the frontier league was stretched beyond "standard" in this land where it was paced by the fleetest of horses on plains and level basin lands.[6]

Mining and stock raising were pursuits of such deep tradition and basic techniques that frontier circumstances could not alter them radically. But confrontation with the Naked Ones was a strange new life-and-death matter that did much to change ways and attitudes. As already indicated, the Chichimecas, in their primitivity and distinctive warfare, were a perennial fear-inducing shock to the frontiersmen of all bloods and mixtures.

Changes in the frontier people wrought by the Chichimeca War and Peace can hardly be overemphasized, and this is particularly true of the quick transformation from the bold individualism of Conquest goals and attitudes to the far less heroic pleading for government help. Every imaginable kind of person entered the Chichimeca Frontier except a "fighting class." There was no order of knighthood and not even an *encomendero* class, as in the south, committed to tutelary protection or Crown military service. Thus it was that the frontier people petitioned for Crown aid and welcomed governmental responsibility for defense, thereby changing fundamentally the ways of imperial expansion in North America.

Even so, frontier residents had to depend much on their own resources to save lives and property: inns and *estancias* kept arms, armed men, and even Indian allies and scouts for defense against Chichimeca attack; homes in exposed mining camps and towns were constructed in special ways to enhance defense capabilities (churches and *conventos* likewise); wagoner-merchants regularly employed armed horsemen as defensive escort; stock ranchers contributed their vaqueros for reprisals against Chichimecas in times of emergency or crisis; frontier towns, in exposed positions, coordinated community arsenals with private arms for defense; and local church or mission bells called the citizenry to armed assembly when there was threat of Indian attack.[7]

Frontier captains, constituting an increasing number of Chichimeca War veterans who were also frontier residents, changed noticeably with their borderlands experience. Intimately acquainted with the war's hardships and dangers and with the nature of the enemy, these veterans were realists who knew that peace must come by means other than perpetual fighting. From the eager slave seekers of earlier years the captains metamorphosed into advocates and practitioners of diplomacy and purchased peace. This was a notable modification, given the cruelties and hatreds of a warfare reaching all categories of population on both sides, but it was also a pragmatic reversion to "old Spanish customs."

When the peace of the 1590s came, these captains and other veteran Chichimeca-fighters were also a reservoir of frontier-toughened colonists ready for the adventures of Nueva Vizcaya and

New Mexico. Some were engaged in the peacemaking itself, as captain-protectors of newly pacified Chichimecas or as teachers of husbandry for the neophytes. Such men, in tandem with the institutions of the new kind of peace fitted to a strange war, helped create precedents that buttressed expansion to farther frontiers.

More significant were the changes in racial and cultural makeup. In this "melting pot" sophisticated nations of the south, often strangers to each other, came together in colonizing and other enterprises in an unknown land. Here they inevitably intermingled with non-Indians, mestizos, mulattoes, zambos, and, of course, pacified Chichimecas. In short, the Chichimeca Frontier was a convergence of the many bloods, classes, and cultural levels that have gone into the making of Mexicans. This borderland medley was not at all the simplistic opposition of Spaniards and Indians that common, but uninformed, opinion puts under the heading of "Spanish Conquest."

This racial-cultural potpourri, this very human *olla podrida*, was, like the northward migration itself, a "manifest destiny." As the frontier people intermingled and raised progeny, they produced a breed seasoned in the wilderness and in enemy action, the beginning of hardiness for farther horizons. This mixture and migration eventually embraced continental distances commensurate to the Anglo-American westward movement—from Querétaro to Alta California's San Francisco approximates the stretch from the Alleghenies to the Pacific Coast. The expansion begun on the sixteenth-century frontier became a single-direction destiny as basic to Mexicans as was the westward march for Anglo-Americans. And this "pull of the North" still influences Mexico, just as the strength of the western magnet continues to drain, and increasingly influence, the eastern United States.

Despite the significance of this centuries-long expansion, the theme is comparatively ignored in Mexico—little studied and almost disdained. Just as the Anglo East gazes down its older nose at a parvenu West, so does Mexican navel contemplation, concentrated in the Valley of Anáhuac and immediate environs, view the "less civilized" north. Mexicans have not yet looked that way with sufficient interest to mythologize (nationalize?) the centuries of adventurous unfolding, the vast store and variety of human drama, or to use fully this expanding "Mexicanism" in the bruited "search for identity."

The Institutional Frontier

In ways more measurable than the human equation, institutional innovation and change on the Chichimeca Frontier limn the abiding features of this upcountry advance of civilization. Chronologically first, of course, were creation and growth of the frontier mining camp and town, mineral law, and mining methods and practices, all beginning here a period of adjustment to an environment that usually differed much from the southern lands. For example, pervasive lack of water for ore processing led to location of towns more distant from mining discoveries than might otherwise have been the case. Water need determined the site of San Luis Potosí, a dozen difficult miles from the mines sustaining it, and the López-Urdiñola ores out of Mazapil were hauled distantly westward to the ore-refining hacienda and incipient town of Río Grande.

Scarcity and transport delays of mercury, greater difficulties in obtaining slave Negro or other labor, and the high and increasing costs of free labor by comparison with nearer and more abundant labor in the southern country were all factors differentiating the new northern mining from earlier circumstances. And mining necessity, more than the demands of war, made this borderland a breeding ground and technique-refining home of the mule pack train, along with the multiple-mule-team wagons plying between Mexico City and Zacatecas and on to New Mexico—prototypes of the later, more famous, twenty-mule teams of California history.

The whole subject of mining change—stock raising, transport, technical factors, commercial activity, governmental facets, labor, social elements, and so on—is still an open field for the investigator, as is the mining, so to speak, of all this human performance for literary and other artistic purposes. Very many of the stories and fictional (or even historical) characters achieving fame in the recent Anglo-American West have a close counterpart somewhere in the earlier centuries of the Spanish-Mexican North.

Similarly, there is a wide field for exploration in the characteristics of governmental development, especially as affected by distance, by jurisdictional clashes and feuds (for example, Mexican versus Guadalajara *Audiencias* and *patria chica* rivalries), and by frontier "scofflawism." Some of this government development is known from the more familiar eighteenth century, a fact that highlights our relative inattention to the first frontier and the seventeenth century. Such neglect also inhibits our understanding of the origins and early growth of those famous borderlands creations, the mission and the presidio.

Missions and presidios, as North American frontier institutions, were born in the Gran Chichimeca. In both cases, the establishments of the first frontier differed, in important ways, from better-known later versions. Thus, the seminal essay by Herbert Eugene Bolton on the Spanish mission as a frontier institution was primarily based on seventeenth- and eighteenth-century examples; the sixteenth-century prototype differed markedly from that later flowering.[8]

Missionary effort, primarily Franciscan, began on the fringes of the Chichimeca Arc, in Michoacan-Querétaro-Jalisco country, in the 1530s and '40s. From then until the peace of the 1590s, missionizing among Chichimecas was largely a failure, with none of the famed successes of subsequent centuries. The Chichimecas were consistently intransigent in a hostility that contained strong signs of anti-Christianity. These *infieles* were notable in their targeting of friars for ridicule, torture, and killing and in similar addiction to the raiding of peaceful Indians who leaned toward, or accepted, Christianity.

Over and above idiomatic difficulties—the multiplicity of dialects and languages that plagued the padres all the way from Querétaro to Alta California and from Nayarit to eastern Texas—Chichimecan hostility dampened missionary fervor with repeated martyrdoms, usually attributable to lack of military protection. Since the military themselves were not fully successful in frontier defense, it is hardly surprising that the missionaries fared so badly. Even had there been imperial imperatives for stronger military support—such as the English, French, and Russian threats in later years—Chichimeca fighting proficiency and unyielding hostility would surely have doomed the missionaries to a minuscule harvest,

at least until there was a sufficiency of captains wise in frontier circumstances. As it was, missionary gain in the Gran Chichimeca had
to wait upon the diplomatic success of the captains beginning in the
late eighties.

One often gets a contrary impression from the writings of the
religious chroniclers, Franciscan and Jesuit. Their complaints about
soldiery, and their firm adherence to the illusion that they were the
only truly effective peacemakers among the heathen (if only there
were no soldiers in sight!), foster, to this day, a disproportionate
sympathy for the mission padres by comparison with the military;
the chroniclers and their modern followers have had all the best of
it in what we now call "public relations." More extensive study of
archival materials, especially revealing of the secular side of things,
is needed to balance such judgments for the sixteenth century in
ways that Professor Bolton did for later "mission" borderlands.

A worthy example of this kind of corrective is the Conde de
Monterrey frontier investigation (*visita*) detailing the Chichimeca
Peace. Here, in hundreds of thousands of words not written for
public consumption, it is abundantly clear that the peace was made
possible and effective by captains instead of friars and that royal
policy purposefully placed the diplomacy of pacification in military
hands, with friars required to attend this governmental gift-giving
so that Chichimeca affection thus gained might "rub off" on them,
too, and facilitate their propagation of the Word. The frontier Chief
Justice, Captain Miguel Caldera, not only structured and supervised the diplomatic gift-giving but was also in charge of *convento*
(mission) construction and friar protection. In the *visita* itself there
is some indication that the friars did not always appreciate this "sec-
ond-fiddle" role; given the friar-Crown tensions of the sixteenth
century's second half, this is not surprising.[9]

The frontier presidio in North America, as noted, began its
long and important history at the outset of the Martín Enríquez
administration. This governor had hardly settled in Mexico City
when he ordered construction of seven presidios, forts with garrisons, to protect the Silver Highway to Zacatecas.

So notable was this innovation that it was immortalized in verse
by New Spain's poet laureate, Fernán González de Eslava, under
the title: "Of the Seven Forts that Viceroy Don Martín Enríquez

Ordered Built, with Garrisons of Soldiers, on the Road That Goes from the City of Mexico to the Mines of Zacatecas, to End the Damage Which the Chichimecas Do to Merchants and Travelers on That Highway." The poet's clarification of his theme forms a subtitle: "The author of this colloquy uses these seven forts to symbolize the Holy Sacrament of the Eucharist; to show that those who travel this world to reach the mines of Heaven, find refuge in these Sacraments, where they are safe against the enemies of the soul."[10] I know of no other presidios, or presidio systems or chains, given such literary recognition, and this is as it should be, for the Enríquez forts were the beginning.

The presidio on this frontier was masonic, usually adobe, with a garrison of three or more men under a *caudillo** or captain. A captain might be in charge of two or more forts when they were grouped closely enough that he could conveniently control them. Occasionally, the term *presidio* meant garrison only, as in a well-established town or city (for example, Guanajuato).

It is a strong indication of the presidio's value that within some fifteen years of the Enríquez start there were fifty or more such establishments on the Chichimeca Frontier. By comparison, northern New Spain's presidios in the late eighteenth century usually numbered but thirty or so. True, later presidios were often larger and more complex than those of the first frontier, but the sheer quantity of these forts and garrisons on a frontier much smaller than the later borderlands underscores the seriousness of the Chichimeca War and the respect accorded it by the viceregal government.

Even by later standards, the presidio of the Gran Chichimeca was not always a small construction. The description of the one at Jalpa, in 1576, says that it is "of size to enclose all the pack animals (*arrias o recuas*) that might arrive, even to the number of more than two hundred, and all the travelers and necessary soldiers."[11] Some of the main presidios, such as those on the heavily traveled *Camino Real de la Tierra Adentro*, were of similar or greater capacity; today's remains of the fort at Nieto Pass, a bit north of Querétaro, certainly indicate this.

These archetypal presidios have not yet received sufficient rec-

*Less than captain, approximately our rank of master sergeant.

ognition of their societal roles in the continent's history. Inevitably, the presidios served needs other than military. Travelers and soldiers tightly packed in such isolated forts certainly engaged in all manner of intercourse, including news-spreading, story telling, just plain gossip, disease transmission, grumbling against the imperial bureaucracy, or whatnot. Trading (including that of contraband) doubtless took place, as also did religious activity, gambling, brawling, criminality, and biological perpetuation—some of most anything human beings engage in. But the presidios were also very visible evidence of a distant king's efforts on behalf of his vassals, thus strengthening, surely, that loyalty to the Crown which cemented the empire for centuries while momentarily bonding against common danger. These presidios cannot be ignored in any serious contemplation of the birth and growth of the Mexican *norteño*.

Here also, in the Gran Chichimeca of those early years, was created, as concomitant of the presidios, a frontier militia—government pay for short-term soldiers and captains recruited solely in New Spain—the first of its kind in North America. This soldiery was created for escort of wagon trains through *tierra de guerra*; inter-presidio patrolling, scouting, and reprisal raids (*entradas*); and presidio garrisoning.

The life of these frontier soldiers was notoriously hard. The men endured low pay; the need to furnish their own horses and costly equipment (usually inadequate); sleeping on the ground in open country (if there was a tent, it was the captain's); risk of wounds, death, or, worst of all, capture and mutilative torture and scalping; and the frequent ill will of other frontier people, either in criticism of a job done or for objectionable behavior in settled areas (for example, gambling away military equipment or failure to pay debts). Death and desertions took heavy toll in the frontier soldiery. But such service could also mean advancement for the durable ones; out of the common soldiery came many of the captains and *alcaldes mayores*,* and sometimes a general.

The Chichimeca Peace of the 1590s is undeservedly unknown to most scholars and frontier buffs. Its institutional construction shows the results of a frontier wisdom learned "the hard way" in preceding

*Provincial judge, usually also with military jurisdiction.

decades. The fact that this kind of pacification was repeated over and over in Spanish-Mexican parts of the continent, wherever primitive, nomadic, and hostile Indians were encountered, seems to affirm its practicality.

Saddle diplomacy, the process of powwow and palaver among the wilderness rancherias to gain Chichimeca acceptance of peace, gifts, settlement on lands suitable for agriculture, and tutelary protection, was the responsibility of the king's captains under a frontier-wide authority exercised by the mestizo Captain Miguel Caldera. Captains specifically commissioned "protectors" of the newly pacified and settled Chichimecas attended to the regular distribution of gifts and rations of food and clothing. These captains also protected the new *gente del rey* ("the king's people," their official designation) against Chichimecas still hostile or against mistreatment or molestation by others of the frontier people, Spanish, Indian, Negro, or mixed. This institutional pattern was called *Protectoría*.

Captain-protectorship had roots in the *encomienda* concept of Peninsular Reconquest and its variant in a New World environment. In the Chichimeca Peace, the captain-protectors played a role similar to that of the *encomenderos* in lands of sedentary, more culturally advanced, Indian nations. They protected their new charges, saw to their sustenance and general well-being, attended to their Christianization by aiding and protecting the missions and friars placed among the neophytes, and led the newly pacified ones as military allies in emergencies, such as threatened or actual war by those still hostile or in rebellion. In such duties the captain-protectors strengthened ties of respect, admiration, and even affection with the newly incorporated Chichimeca chiefs and warriors.

A notable demonstration of this system was the prompt and eager volunteering of the Guachichiles to serve as fighters against the rebellious ones of San Andrés, in the western sierras, in 1592. With three of their own captains already named Miguel Caldera, they gladly enrolled under Chief Justice Caldera to quash the uprising. Viceroy Velasco expressed much satisfaction with this Guachichil "patriotism" in behalf of the frontier peace.

The title of captain-protector continued on in San Luis Potosí, a province embracing and bordering wilderness mountain and tropical country until the eighteenth-century creation of Nuevo Santander and pacification of Sierra Gorda country. In 1783–84, Viceroy Matías de Gálvez, planning government for the western city of Colotlán as a frontier bastion facing untamed rancherias in the western sierras, considered "re-establishing the position of Captain-Protector, as it earlier had been, with the role of Justice and Government, Political and Military."[12] This might be called a bicentennial bow to the deeds of the continent's first great half-breed frontiersman, Miguel Caldera, for this same Colotlán had always been deep in his affections as home of a beloved half-sister and headquarters for his quelling of the San Andrés uprising.

Similarly basic to the Chichimeca Peace was the concept of *proveeduría*: regular governmental supply—through the captain-protectors—of food and clothing plus utensils for cooking, sewing, and farming. Such ministration was intended to sustain the *gente del rey* for some years while they learned to support themselves. What would today be called a humane government "handout" was, in the Chichimeca Peace structure, a purchase of frontier peace with financial outlay much smaller than had been needed for war—a "handout" designed to end bloodletting for Chichimecas and frontier people alike. This government largess was enlightened self-interest, an "aid to underdeveloped nations" while they were being helped toward civilized living, a precocious brand of "corn Christianism," luring the infidels to the civilization and Christianization that were synonymous terms in the European mind of that day.

In some outlying areas of the Chichimeca Frontier, *proveeduría* continued for many years after the peace, sometimes stimulated by Chichimeca threats of alternative return to hostility and isolated ranchería living. And *proveeduría*, as peacemaking and peace keeping, became standard frontier equipment for the remainder of the Spanish Empire period, often used with accompanying amnesties and *protectoría* to placate such farther nations as Apaches, Comanches, Seris, Pimas, and Sibubapas.

Closely linked with these protective and provisioning processes was training of the incoming Chichimecas in the basic arts of sedentary, civilized life. The most urgent and fundamental phase of this, training in agriculture, was entrusted to soldier veterans of the Chichimeca War, who were titled *labradores* and given government salaries to teach the neophytes. This *labrador* system fit well with certain other frontier realities: it established a close personal relationship with the captain-protectors, a quasi-military continuation that was easily understood and respected by the Chichimecas; it was a valuable aid to the relatively few friars, whose hands were filled with the difficulties of teaching Christianity and who, in any case, did not see or appreciate husbandry as one of their primary roles; and it was a sensible and practical way of giving worthy employment to disbanded veterans. The *labrador* system was the genesis of a frontier practice that lived to reach the eighteenth- and nineteenth-century frontier of Upper California, where, in a practice by then long entrenched, presidio soldiers assigned to mission protection served as teachers of husbandry to primitive Indians.

The royal government's insistence that the nearest friars attend gift-giving and ration-giving sessions of the peace—a practice labeled *Intervención*—was, in effect, an effort to stimulate a missionary enterprise hitherto unfruitful. In this sense, as we have seen, the Chichimeca Peace was a large step in making the mission a successful frontier institution, prototype and harbinger of better days to come. And in another precedent for subsequent missionary times the viceregal government shipped northward reading primers in Christian doctrine "for the provisioning of the royal crops for Chichimecas"[13]—a peculiar wording that might have been an accounting convenience (the primers were shipped with agricultural supplies). Perhaps more likely, this mixture of corn-planting tools with reading primers specifically aimed at Chichimeca children might have purposefully expressed the elemental interrelationships of the several parts of the peace process. The primers themselves were a worthy attempt to reach beyond the practicalities of mere subsistence.

One other significant and enduring cornerstone of the Chichimeca Peace was royally sponsored settlement of nearly a thousand Tlaxcalans (690 married, 187 children, and 55 unmarried or widowed, for a total of 932) among several strategic frontier sites. In return for extensive privileges (such as titles of nobility, tax exemptions, concessions pertaining to lands and stock, carrying Spanish arms, and riding horses), the Tlaxcalans were to establish homes and agricultural and pastoral enterprises near the new Chichimeca settlements and were to serve as exemplary practitioners of civilization's ways.

This Tlaxcalan trek and frontier colonization was not entirely original in concept, for similar viceregal sponsorship of advanced Indian cultures for defensive and tutelary settlement in the north had been planned and sometimes effected, on smaller scale, during the Chichimeca War. But the Tlaxcalan enterprise was the greatest and most successful of these efforts, and it was of major importance for subsequent frontier history. Descendants of these first Tlaxcalan pioneers multiplied and were used in similar fashion on farther frontiers, as in Texas and New Mexico. In seventeenth- and eighteenth-century colonization plans, Tlaxcalans were aimed at such distant places as Pensacola and were used for taming the Wichitas in upper Texas and Oklahoma. The practice was common enough that the word "Tlaxcalan" came to be virtually synonymous with Indian frontier colonist, whether of that blood or not, or mixed.

The success of Tlaxcalan frontier planting in the 1590s also lived on in the transplanting of other Indian nations for the same purposes. Thus, Tarascans went into Jalisco, Sinaloa, and Sonora. As those of later frontiers were civilized and Christianized, they, in turn, were sent to farther places as exemplars and teachers: Opatas of southern Sonora into Arizona to teach Pimas, and Indians of Baja California into Alta California. In short, just as the earliest *conquistadores* profited from the aid of Indian allies to triumph over other Indians, so did the Spanish Crown establish an enduring frontier practice of taming hostile primitives by the use of Indian colonist-teachers, until this became "an Old Spanish custom."

In the vast New World stage, the half-century of Spanish-Mexican northward advance after 1546 set an enduring pattern for the successive frontiers that extended Castilian Crown sovereignty until it stretched over about half of the North American continent. In these five or six decades, Spain's ingrained centuries of frontiering, from the mountains and flatlands of Asturias-León and the Duero to the mountains and plains encasing Granada, were revived and renewed in the strangeness of the Mexican lands and peoples. Issuing from a former Aztec hegemony and a new-fledged Castilian sovereignty, these later Spanish frontiersmen, always in company with native allies and apprentices in this replay of *"moros y cristi-anos,"* carved out and tamed this first of the continental border-lands. In doing so, Spanish-Indian pioneers built homes, capital, roads, commerce, towns, governmental structure—all the basic in-gredients and institutions of civilized living—and a new kind of society that would be Mexican. This first frontier people led the way toward the continent's heart, bequeathing to their descendants a compass whose northward-pointed needle never wavered.

Various half-centuries later there came an end, of course, to most of the institutions that defined this first frontier. This cannot be said, however, of the people created in that land and time; the American-European-African mixture that fought, then civilized, then absorbed the aboriginal Chichimeca, lives today on both sides of the Mexican-United States boundary. On either side of that very thin line, when those of Mexican ancestry seriously seek "roots" and "identities," North America's first frontier will merit their con-templation.

NOTES

1. Scarcity of scholarly attention to Mexico's post-Cortesian half-century ac-counts for much of the general incognizance of this early Spanish-American bor-derland. This neglect has made imperative my reliance upon a voluminous docu-mentation, mostly unprinted, in the archives and libraries of Mexico and Spain. At the end of this essay, I have appended a small note on sources to show the scope of this archival investigation and point out the principal published works bearing on this frontier theme.
   In addition to a few definitions and illustrative references, I give several cita-tions of sources, either to identify quoted material or to exemplify the kinds of manuscript materials that shed light upon this time and place. I use short-form citations if full entry is given in the appended note on sources.
   2. Although my purpose in using the labels "Naked Ones" and "Clothes-Wearers" is surely clear enough, I do, on p. 22, offer some comment on the need for this stylistic simplification.
   3. The literature pertaining to sixteenth-century Spanish debates on "just" war and related subjects is sizable; a convenient and authoritative treatment in English is Lewis Hanke, *The Spanish Struggle for Justice in the Conquest of America* (Bos-ton: Little, Brown, 1965).
   4. Viceroy Velasco to the King, June 5, 1590, Archivo General de Indias (AGI), Audiencia de México, 58–3–11.
   5. The phrase is taken from Herbert Eugene Bolton, "The Mission as a Fron-tier Institution in the Spanish-American Colonies," *American Historical Review*, XXIII (October, 1917): 42–61.

6. "No. 196. Nueva Galicia, Nueva España, Céspedes," Museo Nacional (Mexico City), Sección de Manuscritos.

7. The frontier houses of missionary friars were then called *conventos*, but I use the word "mission" because this accurately defines their purpose and is more familiar to the English-language reader.

8. Bolton, "The Mission as a Frontier Institution." Somewhat parallel in concept is my "Genesis of the Frontier Presidio in North America," *Western Historical Quarterly*, XIII, no. 2 (April, 1982): 125–41.

9. This *visita*, which I call the "Conde de Monterrey Frontier Visita" (CMFV), forms *legajo* 851 of AGI, Contaduría. I have described it at some length in my "Peacemaking on North America's First Fronter," *The Americas*, XVI, no. 3 (January, 1960): 221–50, and, more recently, in my *Mexico's Miguel Caldera*, pp. 244–51, 302.

10. Fernán González de Eslava, *Coloquios espirituales y sacramentales y canciones divinas* (Mexico City, 1610).

11. Licenciado Santiago del Riego to Viceroy Enríquez, August 10, 1576, AGI, Patronato 182, *ramo* 52. For a picture of the model of this presidio, see my *Mexico's Miguel Caldera*, p. 46.

12. María del Carmen Velázquez, *Colotlán: Doble frontera contra los bárbaros* (Mexico City, 1961), p. 7.

13. CMFV, Cuaderno de diferentes papeles, pp. 138–39.

Sources

Manuscripts

Except for provincial, municipal, and some private repositories, the
following are the major collections utilized:

1. Archivo General de la Nación (AGN), Mexico City. The several
   sections containing large quantities of frontier material are General de Parte, Historia, Indios, Mercedes, Ordenanzas, Tierras,
   Reales Cédulas (Duplicados). These sections contain data concerning frontier land grants (for example, for ranching, homesites, inns); all kinds of government regulations (for example, private armament, road building, highway inspections); defensive
   Indian settlement; private and commercial shipments of goods
   (food, clothing, utensils); exploration; and mining properties and
   technical matters.
2. Archivo Histórico de Hacienda (AHH), Mexico City. Treasury
   records, such as enlistments and appointment contracts for frontier soldiery, bonds and contracts of paymasters and bursars for
   the Chichimeca War, contain much detail other than strictly financial; thus, physical descriptions of frontier captains are sometimes included in commissions.
3. Museo Nacional (MNM), Mexico City. The large "Seccion de
   Manuscritos" includes transcripts from Spanish archives. Every
   subject imaginable is included; *inter alia* are local and regional
   descriptions by royal officials.
4. Archivo General de Indias (AGI), Seville. The several sections
   containing quantities of frontier material are Audiencia de Guadalajara, Audiencia de México, Contaduría, Indiferente General,
   and Patronato Real. In these is official correspondence of all kinds,
   service records (*probanzas de méritos*), accounts of explorations,
   treasury records, official investigations, and some maps and plans.
5. Bancroft Library, University of California, Berkeley. This library
   contains the section called "Mexican Manuscripts" and large
   quantities of transcripts and microfilm copies from archives in Spain
   and Mexico.

Printed Documents

The main collections pertaining very specifically to the essay subject are

1. Velázquez, Primo Feliciano, ed. *Colección de documentos para la historia de San Luis Potosí.* 4 vols. San Luis Potosí, 1897–99.
2. Powell, Philip Wayne, ed., and Maria L. Powell, paleographic transcr. *Crescendo of the Chichimeca War, 1551–1585,* vol. 1, *War and Peace on the North Mexican Frontier: A Documentary Record* (Madrid, 1971).

Books

The following works bear entirely, or very importantly, upon the North Mexican frontier in the sixteenth century and are mainly of recent, monographic type. The reader is referred to the bibliographies in these works for additional books and periodical literature.

1. Alessio Robles, Vito. *Francisco de Urdiñola y el norte de la Nueva España.* Mexico City, 1931.
2. Bakewell, Peter J. *Silver Mining and Society in Colonial Mexico: Zacatecas, 1546–1700.* London, 1971.
3. Chevalier, François. *La formation des grands domaines au Mexique: Terre et societé aux XVIe–XVIIe siècles.* Paris, 1952. Spanish edition: *Problemas agrícolas e industriales de México.* Mexico City, 1956. English edition: *Land and Society in Colonial Mexico: The Great Hacienda.* Berkeley, 1963.
4. Dávila Garibi, José Ignacio. *La sociedad de Zacatecas en los albores del régimen colonial: Actuación de los principales fundadores y primeros funcionarios públicos de la ciudad.* Mexico City, 1939.
5. Del Hoyo, Eugenio. *Historia del Nuevo Reino de León (1577–1723).* 2 vols. Monterrey, Mex., 1972.
6. Las Casas, Gonzalo de. *Noticia de los Chichimecas y justicia de la guerra que se les ha hecho por los españoles.* In *Quellen zur Kulturgeschichte des präkolumbischen Amerika,* ed. Hermann Trimborn. Stuttgart, 1936.
7. Mecham, John Lloyd. *Francisco de Ibarra and Nueva Vizcaya.* Durham, N.C., 1927.
8. Powell, Philip Wayne. *Mexico's Miguel Caldera: The Taming of America's First Frontier (1548–1597).* Tucson, 1977. Spanish edition: *Capitán mestizo: Miguel Caldera y la frontera norteña; la pacificación de los chichimecas (1548–1597),* Mexico City, 1980.
9. ———. *Soldiers, Indians and Silver: The Northward Advance of New Spain, 1550–1600.* Berkeley, 1952, 1969; Tempe, Ariz., 1975.

Spanish edition: *La guerra chichimeca (1550–1600)*, Mexico City, 1977.

10. Velázquez, Primo Feliciano. *Historia de San Luis Potosí*. 4 vols. Mexico City, 1946–48.

The Frontiers of New France

FREDERICK JACKSON TURNER, in his seminal essay "The Significance of the Frontier in American History," defined the frontier as
the outer edge of the wave of American westward expansion, lying
at the hither edge of free land. In this frontier zone he saw the
germs of European institutions developing in an American environment. To him the environment was all-important, it was "the line
of most rapid and effective Americanization. . . . Moving westward, the frontier became more and more American," for, as he put
it, "the wilderness masters the colonist." Thus "the advance of the
frontier meant a steady movement away from the influence of Europe, a steady growth of independence on American lines." Turner
saw peculiar institutions developing on this advancing frontier that
profoundly modified and influenced those of the earlier settled regions on the Atlantic Seaboard. In this theory there is an element
akin to the Whig interpretation of British history. The result becomes the cause.

Regardless of the degree of credence granted Turner's hypothesis, there was one frontier in North America to which it did not
apply, namely, the frontier of New France that endured for two
centuries. Turner himself sought vainly to make that frontier fit his
model in his article "The Rise and Fall of New France."[1] A. L. Burt
subsequently sought to demonstrate that the social values and institutions of New France were completely dominated by the frontier environment.[2] Arguments he presented in support of his *a priori*
conclusions are, to say the least, unconvincing.

The Canadian frontier, before the British conquest, was unique.
Unlike the American frontier, it was not a line of settlement, not a
zone that developed original and enduring institutions, but a series
of lines stretching west, north, and south into the wilderness along
the water routes—lines that had length but no breadth. On the

Canadian frontier a peculiar way of life developed which had not a little effect on society in the settlements of the Saint Lawrence Valley; yet the changes that occurred on this frontier and the development of it over time were governed not so much by events and conditions on the frontier itself as by events and decisions made in Europe. To a large degree this frontier, stretching thousands of miles into the heart of the continent, was the frontier not of Quebec and Montreal but of La Rochelle, Bordeaux, and Versailles. Policies and resultant decisions made in the latter places dictated the course of major events on this remote frontier.[3]

Down to 1663 the French crown had little influence on events in America. During those early years private enterprise, fishermen, fur traders, and missionaries established and maintained the French presence, first in Acadia and then far inland in the Saint Lawrence Valley. Agricultural settlements were eventually undertaken merely to protect the fishing, fur trade, and missionary bases and not, be it noted, as the forerunners of an intensive colonization effort. In this regard the French experience differed markedly from that of the Spanish and the English. In Acadia the French were never numerous enough to constitute a threat to the resident Indian peoples. When, in the 1530s and 1540s, they attempted to establish a base on the Saint Lawrence near Quebec, they quickly aroused the enmity of the local Iroquoian tribes and were forced to withdraw. Some seventy years later, when they returned to the site, those tribes were no longer there. It is likely that these Indians had been weakened decades earlier by disease, contracted from Europeans, before being destroyed by the Hurons.[4]

The French, therefore, when they finally established themselves in what came to be called Canada, had no need to dispute with the Indians for possession of the land and no need to purchase it. The land was vacant. In 1616, a quarter-century before Montreal was established, the Algonquians and Hurons, far from opposing the French presence, pleaded with Champlain to establish a post on the island to facilitate trade and provide a secure base for the prosecution of their war with the Iroquois Confederacy.[5] These Indians came periodically to the French settlements to trade their furs and discuss concerted action against the Iroquois, but contact there dwindled once the French had established posts in Huronia.

The Hurons regarded trade in furs not solely as a commercial trans-action but also, and perhaps chiefly, as an exchange of gifts to seal their military alliance. For the French the fur trade, the mainstay of their enterprise in America, demanded that good relations be maintained with the Indian suppliers of furs. By the same token the Indians had to tolerate the French to obtain European goods and military aid. Thus, from the outset on this frontier, trade and war were closely entwined.[6]

When, in 1615, French missionaries arrived to begin their drive to convert all the Indian nations to Christianity, this need for good relations was strengthened. Three-quarters of a century later an-other motive appeared and became the dominant one: namely, An-glo-French imperial rivalry, the belief in the one country that what-ever benefited the other had to be opposed. Armed hostilities that continued for more than thirty of the ensuing seventy-odd years required that the French maintain close economic and military al-liances with the Indian nations to offset the great superiority in numbers enjoyed by the Anglo-Americans. Here, then, was the most distinctive feature of this peculiar Canadian frontier. Whereas the Spanish destroyed some nine-tenths of the Indian population, enslaving the survivors,[7] and the English steadily drove the Indians off their lands until (after the conquest of New France) they were at last able to embark with impunity on a policy of genocide, the French from the outset were dependent on the Indians and dared do nothing that might offend them.

Second only to the role of the Indians in the development of this frontier was geography. In the thirteen English colonies, with one exception the rivers flowing from the Appalachians to the At-lantic were not navigable by ocean-going ships for any great dis-tance—the fall line being close to the coast. The exception was the Hudson River, but access beyond its headwaters to the Great Lakes was blocked by the powerful Five Nations' Confederacy. From the north, at Hudson Bay, through country that was scarce in game, the interior could be reached only by canoe during the short, frost-free season, along rivers flowing from the west. Food supplies had to be transported inland through a wide zone that came to be known as the "starving country." Thus, after establishing itself on the shores of the bay in 1670, the Hudson's Bay Company made only one at-

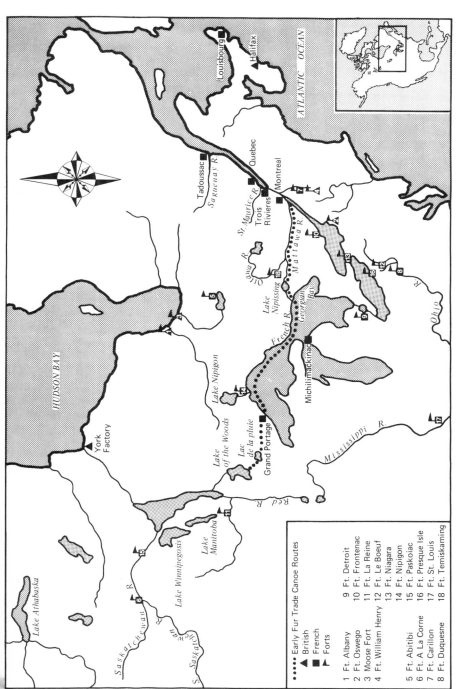

Eighteenth Century Canada and its Dependencies

ATLANTIC OCEAN

Louisbourg
Halifax

HUDSON BAY

York Factory

Lake Athabaska

Saskatchewan R.

S. Saskatchewan R.

Lake Winnipegosis

Lake Manitoba

Red R.

Lake of the Woods

Lac de la pluie

Grand Portage

Lake Nipigon

Lake Nipissing

Tadoussac
Saguenay R.
Quebec
St. Maurice R.
Trois Rivieres
Montreal
Ottawa R.
Mattawa R.
French R.
Georgian Bay

Michilimackinac

Mississippi R.

Ohio R.

Early Fur Trade Canoe Routes
British
French
Forts

1 Ft. Albany
2 Ft. Oswego
3 Moose Fort
4 Ft. William Henry
5 Ft. Abitibi
6 Ft. A La Corne
7 Ft. Carillon
8 Ft. Duquesne
9 Ft. Detroit
10 Ft. Frontenac
11 Ft. La Reine
12 Ft. Le Boeuf
13 Ft. Niagara
14 Ft. Nipigon
15 Ft. Paskoiac
16 Ft. Presque Isle
17 Ft. St. Louis
18 Ft. Temiskaming

tempt to penetrate inland before the conquest of New France. That attempt ended in disaster.[8]

The French, at the beginning of the seventeenth century, gained control of the Saint Lawrence, established their main base at Quebec, a thousand miles from the ocean, and from there they had easy access along the Ottawa and Saint Lawrence rivers to the Great Lakes. The watershed between those lakes and the Mississippi was low and short, presenting no transport problem. Similarly, the portage from Lake Superior to the rivers flowing into Lake Winnipeg was easily traversed. From Lake Winnipeg the French could travel along northern rivers to the Rocky Mountains, Hudson Bay, or even the Arctic Ocean had they so desired. At the beginning of the eighteenth century, the French, for reasons of imperial policy, seized the region at the mouth of the Mississippi. This gave them control of the two main watercourses draining the southern half of the continent and with it, control of the whole interior from the western slopes of the Appalachians to the Rocky Mountains. New France could thus be aptly described as a river empire.

To make use of these river routes, some form of water transport was needed, as well as food supplies en route. Here again the French were fortunate. The Indian's birchbark canoe was, until the nineteenth century, the only viable means of transportation. It was easily manufactured with nothing more than an axe, a knife, and an awl. Although light enough to be carried over a portage by one or two men, it could carry a load varying from one thousand to four thousand pounds, depending on its size. Happily for the French, the birch trees that provided the bark for these canoes grew in profusion in areas they controlled but were scarce to the south and nonexistent around Hudson Bay.[9] The French thus acquired control of the rivers of the interior and a monopoly on the craft needed to voyage along them. As for food supplies, again they were lucky. The Saint Lawrence Valley, Great Lakes basin, and plains south of Lake Winnipeg lay on the northern edge of the corn belt. Dried, leached corn was highly nutritious and easily stored and transported. In addition, fish and game abounded. It was therefore no accident that the French had reached the Rocky Mountains while the English were still struggling over the Appalachians.

Unlike the English, the French did not occupy these lands

they traversed. In their frail canoes they were more akin to merchant seamen voyaging across the Atlantic to obtain a cargo at some distant port. Their canoes left no more imprint on the country than did the wake of a sailing ship on the ocean. Theirs, unlike the Anglo-American or the Spanish frontier, was not a frontier of settlement. They did not destroy the forest, driving off the wildlife and the Indians as they advanced; creating farms, roads, towns; changing the whole appearance and function of the land. In the Saint Lawrence Valley there were farms unlike those anywhere else on the continent. The Canadian farms were laid out in long, narrow strips running back from the great river, which was the colony's main and, for many years, only highway. To the observer traveling up the river by boat from Quebec to Montreal, the whole colony came steadily into view like a long, straggling village street, with every few hundred yards a farmhouse and every few miles a parish church.[10] At the rear of these farms was the virgin forest, waiting for future generations of settlers.

In one respect the Canadian frontier fitted the Turner pattern. The abundance of free land had profound effects on Canadian society, making it markedly at variance with the parent society in France and somewhat akin to that of the English colonies. This free land permitted all who desired to become landholders and removed the necessity to work permanently for wages. Yet the comparison with the English colonies cannot be carried too far. One feature notably absent in New France was the village community. Attempts by royal officials to have settlers concentrate their homes and farm buildings in village centers that would be more easily defended and supervised by the authorities met with failure. The settlers, from the outset, insisted on living on their individual strips of land in a dispersed fashion more vulnerable to attack but affording privacy, elbow room, and freedom from surveillance. Economic independence thus bred an independent attitude toward life and toward authority, something that newcomers from France and the royal officials constantly remarked upon.[11] It would, however, be a mistake to attribute this characteristic to the availability of free land alone. A major cause was the Canadians' relative affluence, to which free land notably contributed, but another equally important factor was the absence of taxation in New France. Whereas a French peasant paid out between one-third and one-half of his produce and earnings in feudal dues, taxes, and tithe,[12] the Canadians paid less than 10 percent in seigneurial dues, and their tithe was half that levied in northern France.[13]

This edge of settlement was certainly a frontier, of sorts—one that still exists today—but its only denizens were small bands of nomadic Indian hunters. It was not a frontier zone where two different peoples met, mingled, or clashed. On the northern horizon was the ragged line of the Laurentian mountains stretching to the sub-Arctic tundra, and to the south was the edge of the Appalachians, with the Saint Lawrence flowing majestically through the alluvial plain. Down that river the fur traders' canoes brought something of the western frontier to the doorsteps of most of the homes in the colony.

Inevitably, from the earliest days this river pulled the French westward, first from Quebec to an outpost at Trois Rivières to drain the furs of the northern hinterland at the head of the Saint Maurice River, then with a great leap forward to a missionary and fur trading base established among the Huron tribes on the shores of Georgian Bay. This jump was followed, in 1642, by the establishment of a major missionary settlement at Montreal. It was at these two mission centers, Sainte-Marie-des-Hurons and Montreal, that a curious form of frontier developed, a religious frontier of the intellect, where first the Recollets and then the Jesuits struggled to convert the Indians to Christianity and to persuade them to adopt the European way of life.[14]

The preamble to the chapter of the Company of One Hundred Associates, founded by Cardinal Richelieu in 1627, stated that the main purpose of the Company was to assist in the conversion of the Indian nations to Christianity. Article seventeen of the charter declared that the descendants of the French who settled permanently in the colony, and also those Indians who became practicing Christians, would be regarded as French subjects. As such they could take up residence in France whenever they wished and there acquire, bequeath, and succeed to property and accept grants and legacies just as could any other of the king's subjects, without the need to obtain naturalization papers.[15] That no North American Indians ever sought to avail themselves of this privilege does not detract from the well-meaning intent of the French Crown. When in 1640 a large part of the island of Montreal was granted to the Seminary of Saint Sulpice, the opening sentence of the patent stated, "Our greatest desire being to establish a strong colony in New France in order to instruct the wild peoples of those regions in the knowledge of God and to bring them to a civil way of life. . . ."[16] Montreal was thus the only city in the New World established solely to serve the Indian people.

The attempt was, however, a failure. The Jesuits eventually succeeded in grasping the basic tenets of the Hurons' religious beliefs and came to accept that much they had first condemned as vicious—as the work of Satan—was in fact innocent and reconcilable with Christian teaching, yet they insisted on striving to have the Indians reject much that was basic to their entire way of life. The priests strove continually to assimilate the Indians. The Hurons resented these efforts and would have driven the Jesuits out had it not been that the Company of One Hundred Associates made the continued presence of the missionaries a condition of trade: no missionaries, no more trade goods. On one point the Jesuits were adamant: only those who had been baptized and who lived according to Christian precepts in this world could enjoy eternal life in the next. The Indians were appalled by the notion that those who became Christian would be cut off after death from the family members who remained true to their old beliefs and from their ancestors. The struggle was thus extended beyond the last frontier of all. When one member of a family accepted Christianity, the others were inclined to follow suit merely to preserve the family unit intact after death. Eventually a majority in a few villages were converted, and converts from other villages joined them, while those who chose to remain pagan had to remove themselves. The Huron nation became divided.

When disease of European origin swept through the Huron villages, wiping out half the population, the black-robed priests were held responsible, as indeed they likely but inadvertently were. Villagers, weakened and divided among themselves, fell easy prey to the savage onslaughts of the better-armed Iroquois Confederacy. The Huron Nation was destroyed, and only a few scattered remnants were left.[17] The great experiment had failed. It had proven

impossible to assimilate the Indians. The only persons to be assim-
ilated were some young French fur traders, who, to the dismay of
the Jesuits, adopted the Indian way of life.

The French learned a great deal from the Indians; they could
not have survived in the environment without that acquired knowledge. They adopted some items of Indian clothing, canoes, snow-
shoes, and toboggans. The French also accepted some Indian values; they, too, became supremely stoical and, like the Indians,
revered personal bravery and hardihood above all. They showed a
fierce independence of spirit and a marked disinclination to abide
by prudent bourgeois or peasant values.[18] Yet too much should not
be made of this cultural adaptation, for the Canadians still remained
distinctly European. The laws and institutions that governed their
lives were those of France modified to a degree to suit local conditions. Their religion was purely that of Rome. Similarly, society in
the settlements showed no influence of the Indians' permissive sexual mores. Indians viewed an unmarried girl as mistress of her own
body with the right to sleep with any man she chose. When among
the Indians, Frenchmen freely availed themselves of the opportunities thus presented. Yet this acceptable practice had no perceiv-
able influence on the mores of the Canadians at home.[19] There,
premarital chastity was the norm, adultery was regarded as a crime,
and every effort was made to conceal lapses from the accepted standards.

The system of government remained the paternal autocracy of
France. Only at a parish level was there any trace of democracy,
but this was the village democracy of the mother country. The much-
vaunted democracy of the Anglo-American frontier was conspicuous by its absence.[20] Also lacking was the frontier spirit of egalitarianism. Society in both the settlements and in the west was distinctly
hierarchical, status-ordered, and dominated by the nobility, who
held 53 percent of the seigneuries, the senior posts in the administration, and who controlled the fur trade.[21]

Nor did the casual anarchy of the Indian villages have any discernible influence on society in the French settlements. The rule
of French law was accepted in the colony and on the frontier, although the Indians could never be brought to submit to it. The
word *civilized* had not yet come into use in either the French or

English languages, but the French made a distinction between an ordered society living under the rule of law, that is, *policé*, and a society without laws, or *sauvage*.[22] The French always referred to the Indians as *les sauvages*, but the word cannot be translated as "savages." As the French of the seventeenth and eighteenth centuries used the term, it had no pejorative meaning; it merely meant wild or free as opposed to domesticated or subject to man-made coercive laws.

The French were acutely aware of the basic difference between their attitude towards communal life and that of the Indians. They noted the obvious and, to them, astonishing degree of personal freedom enjoyed by the Indians. Every Indian man was his own master, accountable for his actions to no one but himself and the needs of his family; the concept of private property or the accumulation of surplus wealth had no meaning. An eighteenth-century Jesuit historian, Pierre-François-Xavier de Charlevoix, who had spent some years at Quebec and subsequently voyaged through the west to New Orleans, expressed quite cogently the dilemma that the Indians' concept of freedom and polity posed for the French:

> In one word these American Indians are perfectly convinced that man is born free, that no power on earth has the right to attack their liberty, and that nothing could compensate them for the lack of it. On this point it has not been easy to disabuse the Christians [Indians] and make them understand that as a result of the corruption of our nature, manifested by way of sin, unrestrained freedom to do bad, differs little from a sort of necessity to commit it, in view of the inclination that sweeps us towards it. The law that restrains us brings us back to our basic liberty while appearing to deprive us of it.[23]

Charlevoix did, however, qualify this declaration by admitting that the Indians with their simpler appetites, and by internalized restraint, were able to cope with freedom much more easily than could Europeans. Judging from the attitudes and reactions of the Canadians, indeed the whole structure of their society, they agreed with Charlevoix on the need for social coercion.

After the destruction of the Huronia mission, the evangelical drive of the French missionaries was greatly diminished; the age of Jesuit martyrs was over. The clergy now devoted themselves mainly to serving the slowly increasing body of settlers in the Saint Lawrence Valley. Mission posts were established throughout the Great Lakes basin, but always alongside them were the ubiquitous cabins of the fur traders, and it was the latter who proved to be the greater attraction for the Indians, to the dismay of the clerics.[24] By the mid-seventeenth century the western Canadian frontier had assumed the character it was to retain until the third decade of the nineteenth century.

In 1663, however, when the French Crown took over the administration of New France from the moribund Company of One Hundred Associates, the secretary of state responsible for the colonies, Jean-Baptiste Colbert, sought to prevent French expansion into the west. He laid it down as Crown policy that the limit of settlement was to be the western end of the island of Montreal. No concessions of land were to be granted, or fur trade posts established, beyond that point. The meager French population was to be concentrated along the Saint Lawrence downstream from Montreal, there to devote itself to agriculture in order to make the colony self-sufficient in foodstuffs and to engage in such industries as lumbering, shipbuilding, fishing, and the exchange of Canadian goods for West Indies tropical produce and French manufactured wares. Furs were not to be neglected, but the French settlers were not to be allowed to voyage to the west in search of them; instead, the Indians were to bring their furs to Montreal to trade.[25] In short, he wanted New France to play the same mercantilist role in the French empire as the thirteen colonies played in that of England.

Despite his best efforts, including stringent laws that could invoke the death penalty, it proved impossible to prevent the French from voyaging west to forestall the competition. Every year a few hundred defied the edicts and left the colony to travel to the distant Indian villages and obtain the pick of the furs. These were the famous *coureurs de bois*.[26] They were able to earn in one summer more than could be gained in five years of back-breaking labor clearing a few acres of virgin forest to raise a subsistence crop. In addition, the imbalance of the sexes was a powerful motive for men to abandon the land for a roving life in the west. To establish a viable farm, a wife was a necessity; children were the only source of labor, the only security for the future. Yet during these years the shortage of women in the colony meant that only one man in six

could hope to find a wife. Not until the second decade of the eighteenth century were the sexes in balance.[27] Moreover, Indian girls
were comely and their sexual mores very permissive.[28] Thus, despite the Royal edicts, French penetration of the west continued
throughout the basin of the Great Lakes and beyond.

These fur traders, once they had left the confines of the settlements, did not cast off all the trammels of civilization. They still
remained subject to the laws of the colony and the regulations en-
acted by the officials at Quebec and Montreal as the need arose,
frequently on direct orders of the minister of marine. The long arm
of the government at Versailles reached far out into the wilderness.
The main instrument of control was the *congé*, or license. The *congé*
system was first introduced in 1681 by Jean-Baptiste Colbert in an
attempt to reduce the number of *coureurs de bois* and curb the
drain on the labor supply desperately needed to clear the land and
bring it into production. In 1696 a temporary glut of beaver pelts
that had flooded the European market caused the minister to revoke the *congés*.[29] In 1716 they were reintroduced, revoked again
in 1720, and reinstituted in 1726.

The original *congé* system was simple enough; the governor-
general was authorized to issue twenty-five permits a year, each
one allowing a canoe with three men to go to the west to trade. By
order of the king permits were to be granted without charge to the
poorer families and to charitable institutions, such as hospitals. The
recipients could then sell them to fur traders, the usual price in the
1680s being one thousand *livres*, the equivalent of fifty pounds sterling. The intention here was that the permits would serve as a form
of relief for the poor. The individual who actually made use of the
congé had to register it with the authorities at Montreal before de-
parting for the west and give the names of the men paddling the
canoe. In this way, it was hoped, not more than seventy-five men
would be out of the colony at a time, and the authorities would
know who was legally in the west.[30]

In the eighteenth century canoes used in the trade became
bigger, carrying loads of up to four thousand pounds and requiring
crews of five to twelve men. The number of canoes going west was
limited not by an arbitrary edict but by the needs of the trade and
military policy. The governor-general issued as many *congés* as he

deemed appropriate, selling them by auction to the highest bidder and using the proceeds for charitable purposes.[31]

Another effective instrument of control over the voyageurs who paddled the canoes for wages was their *engagement,* or contract. In the eighteenth century hundreds of these *engagements* were drawn up by the notaries of Montreal every year. They stated the name of the voyageur, the parish where he resided, the name of the fur trader hiring him, frequently the post where he was to go (unfortunately for the historian, some notaries merely wrote in *pays d'en haut,* which meant virtually anywhere in the west), and when he was to return, whether that same summer or a year or two hence. The voyageur's duties and responsibilities were carefully spelled out along with the wages and fringe benefits that he was to receive. Every such contract declared that the voyageur could not quit his master's service before its completion and that he had to obey all honest and legal orders. The penalty for noncompliance was forfeiture of the stipulated wages, which were not paid until the voyageur returned to Montreal.[32]

Voyageurs were thus obliged to behave in as seemly a manner in the west as in the central colony. Military commandants at the western posts also saw to it that the voyageurs did not get out of hand. It was not just the economically disadvantaged, the illiterate semicivilized, who lived on this frontier. There, too, the colonial nobility maintained a dominant role.[33] Occasionally a troublemaker was sent back to Montreal under armed escort to be dealt with by the authorities. Even in civil matters men who went to the west and failed to live up to their contractual obligations could be brought to account by a complaint to a post commandant, who would see to it that the offender was sent back to Montreal with the autumn convoy.[34] In addition, at the main posts were chaplains who could exert considerable pressure by denying absolution to any men who flouted the moral laws of the church. This frontier was anything but lawless; it was not a zone where the Canadians were free of the normal restraints of their society.[35]

Trading posts were established at the eastern end of Lake Ontario, at Niagara, on the Illinois River, at Michilimackinac, on both sides of Lake Superior, and on the shores of Hudson Bay and James Bay. When, in 1689, William of Orange seized the throne of En-

gland and brought the kingdom into the coalition of powers struggling to curb Louis XIV's aggressive foreign policy, New France was
assaulted by the English colonies and their Iroquois allies. The Canadians were able to repel these assaults and, by enlisting the aid
of their Indian fur trade partners, to carry the war to the enemy.
War also provided the means to expand the volume of the fur trade.
New posts with military garrisons were established throughout the
west at the Crown's expense, ostensibly to provide arms and supplies to the Indian allies, but in reality to garner furs.[36]

This development was to have a profound effect on Canadian
society. Officers appointed to command these western posts gained
control of the fur trade.[37] At the same time the officer corps of these
colonial regulars, the *Troupes de la Marine*, came increasingly to
be drawn from the ranks of the Canadian seigneurs until eventually
they formed a military caste.[38] Moreover, the Canadian labor force
in the trade, the voyageurs who transported the trade goods to the
Indians, lived in their villages for months on end, accompanied their
war parties, and brought the furs back to Montreal, thereby gained
the training needed for forest warfare. Out of necessity, they became the finest guerrilla fighters in America. The fur trade was to
the Canadian military establishment what the Atlantic fisheries were
to the naval powers of Europe, a vital training ground and manpower reserve to be drawn on in time of war. War and the fur trade
were thus inextricably joined.

The short-term economic consequences of this expansion of the
fur trade under the guise of military operations were, however, ca-
lamitous. Beaver fur was the mainstay of the trade, being used in
the manufacture of felt hats. The amount being exported from Canada to France came to exceed the market requirements some five
times over. The Company of the Farm, which had purchased from
the French Crown the lease of trading privileges in the colonies,
the Africa slave trade, tropical produce of the Antilles, beaver pelts
and moose hides of New France (for one-half million *livres* a year),
would see profits greatly reduced by its losses in the Canada trade.[39]
It could not be expected to renew a lease under those conditions,
and the Crown could not afford to lose that source of revenue.

In 1696 the minister of marine, Louis Phélypeaux de Pontchartrain, felt obliged to take drastic action. He ordered the suspension

of all trade in beaver pelts and the abandonment of all but one post in the west; Fort Saint-Louis-des-Illinois was to be retained for purely military purposes. Colonial officials and the Canadian fur trading community were aghast when the order was received. The governor-general and the intendant at Quebec wrote at great length pleading for a reversal of the edict. They declared that to withdraw from the west in this fashion, while the colony was engaged in a bitter war with the English and their Iroquois allies, could well prove fatal. It would be an open invitation to the enemy to occupy the abandoned posts. Then a desperate and hideously expensive military campaign would have to be mounted to oust them; otherwise the western nations would all be drawn into the English camp and New France would be doomed.[40]

Pontchartrain was constrained to cancel his edict, thus making it obvious that France was irrevocably committed to the maintenance of its tenuous hold on the interior of the continent even though the economic benefits to be derived from the vast region were, at the time, negligible. The commercial frontier of fur-trade posts linked by the water routes had thus become primarily a military and political frontier that had to be maintained regardless of cost. Three years later, in 1700, on the eve of renewed Anglo-French hostilities, Louis XIV incorporated this western military frontier as a basic feature of French imperial policy. Settlements were to be established at Detroit and at the mouth of the Mississippi, forts were to be established down the length of that river, and all the Indian nations from the Great Lakes to the Gulf of Mexico were to be secured in an alliance to bar the English colonials from the territory west of the Alleghenies. The English were to be kept hemmed in between the Atlantic and the eastern slope of the mountains.[41] Missionaries, now become agents of French imperialism, were dispatched to the Mississippi valley to assist the military and the fur traders in holding all the Indian nations in a close alliance. Fur traders had to supply them with the goods they needed, and if this could not be done at a profit, then it had to be done with the aid of Crown subsidies.[42] Religion and commerce both had to serve the one end—that of the new French imperial policy. The whole fabric and purpose of the French presence in the west, on this peculiar frontier, had undergone a radical change. From this point on, the

Canadian frontier was merely the western limit of the new French Empire. The Indian nations were to be treated as French allies and clients to contain the English in just the same way that Poland and certain of the German states were used to contain the Hapsburg Empire in central Europe.

There were, however, two sides to this frontier, two peoples involved. To date it has been viewed only from the one side, that of the French. The questions still must be asked: How did this frontier, this zone where two cultures (Indian and French) met, look to the Indians? What hypotheses would an Indian Turner or Webb have conceived to explain what was transpiring and the consequences it would have for the Indian peoples? To the Indians of the north, unlike those facing the English colonists to the south, the French could not have appeared as a sinister force seriously threatening their traditional way of life or their control of their ancestral lands. In 1754 the Mission Iroquois, who a century before had been converted to Christianity by the Jesuits and had removed to New France, put the issue very succinctly:

> Brethren, are you ignorant of the difference between our Father and the English? Go see the forts our Father has erected, and you will see that the land beneath his walls is still hunting ground, having fixed himself in those places we frequent, only to supply our wants; whilst the English, on the contrary, no sooner get possession of a country than the game is forced to leave it; the trees fall down before them, the earth becomes bare, and we find among them hardly wherewithal to shelter us when the night falls.[43]

To the Indian nations on the borderlands of New England the French were a powerful ally, providing them with the means to resist the steady encroachment of English settlement on their lands. From the French point of view the Abenakis, Micmacs, and Malecites served as a buffer to keep the English well back from the Saint Lawrence River, which they had long claimed to be the true frontier between the lands of the English and French crowns.[44] In 1704, Governor-general Vaudreuil persuaded a large band of Abenakis to remove from Acadia to lands ceded to them on the Saint François River south of Quebec and at Bécancour near Trois Rivières to protect the southern approaches to the seigneurial settlements.[45]

In the west the French claimed sovereignty over the entire

continent from the Alleghenies to the Pacific, a claim that the English refused to recognize. In reality the French claim was illusionary, advanced to justify their exclusion of the English. In that time and place it had no meaning for the simple reason that the Indians were still sovereign in all the lands they occupied. They merely tolerated the French at specific points to provide them with the European goods they desired. Maps drawn by cartographers of North America depicting a vast area under French control and, after 1713, a similarly vast area spreading out from Hudson Bay as under British sovereignty are, to say the least, mythical. The British never controlled more than a few isolated points on the uninhabited shores of Hudson Bay. The French, with the exception of small settlements at Detroit and in the Illinois country, on lands not occupied by Indians, never controlled anything in the west beyond the range of their muskets and small cannon at their dispersed forts. Down to the conquest of New France the Indian nations dominated the west.[46] It was in fact their country regardless of the extravagant claims made at Versailles and Westminister.[47] French claims to territorial sovereignty beyond the confines of their actual settlements were, in fact, claims against the English—an attempt to forestall the English rather than a *de facto* usurpation of the Indians' claim to the lands they occupied. English claims to lands they had never even seen were, at the time, no more valid than the English kings' claim to the throne of France, which was not relinquished until 1802, when it was omitted from the preamble to the Treaty of Amiens.

When the French wished to establish a post, they had first to obtain the consent of the Indians in the region. They could maintain these posts only by providing the Indians with the goods and services they required at prices they were willing to pay. Were either the price or the quality to prove unsatisfactory, the Indians had the option (which they exercised frequently enough to keep it viable) of going to the English traders of New York, Pennsylvania or Hudson Bay. The French were much more dependent on the Indians than the latter were on the French, who, so few in numbers, had to rely on the Indians to bar English westward expansion. The main responsibility of the post commanders, carefully spelled out in their official instructions, was to keep the Indians in their respective districts from entering into any negotiations with the English. They also had to strive to keep the various nations at peace with each other.[48] This last was no easy task, since many of these tribes remained in a permanent state of war. To them war was a form of blood sport which allowed their young braves to demonstrate valor and prove their manhood. Casualties had usually been light, but (with the appearance of European fur traders) an economic motive had been added as tribes fought to preserve a privileged position as traders, to deny firearms to their foes, or to gain access themselves to supplies of those new and deadly weapons.

At mid-century one of the more experienced western post commanders, Jacques Le Gardeur de St. Pierre, reported from Lac de la Pluie that, in a meeting he had convened of the Sakis, Puants, and Foxes, he had scant success in his attempts to make them cease warring with the Sioux. He stated that they were extremely recalcitrant, insubordinate, and greedy for gifts and never satisfied with what they were given. The French, clearly, were not masters of the situation. Like all the commandants of the western posts, St. Pierre had orders, emanating from Versailles, to find an overland route to the Pacific Ocean. In his journal of 1750 he described in detail the difficulties he had encountered as he and his men pushed westward along the Saskatchewan River among the warring tribes, now well supplied with horses. To indicate what he had to face, he cited one incident that had occurred at his main base, Fort La Reine on the Assiniboine River. Two hundred armed Assiniboine warriors invaded the fort without warning and made it plain that they intended to kill St. Pierre and his five men, then pillage the fort's supplies. In desperation St. Pierre dashed into the powder magazine, knocked the lid off a keg of gunpowder, seized a brand from a fire, and strode into their midst. Holding the brand over the open keg, he told the warriors their intentions were obvious, but at least he would have the satisfaction of taking them with him. At that they flew for the gate and almost knocked it off its hinges in their haste to get away.[49]

St. Pierre's lieutenant, the chevalier de Niverville, did eventually succeed in establishing a post, Fort La Jonquière, in the foothills of the Rocky Mountains, but the communication route through the lands of the warring Cree, Sioux, and Blackfoot, and the attendant problem of supplies, made it impossible to proceed further or even to sustain the fort.[50] This post marked the final extent of French westward expansion.

When the French sought to subdue a recalcitrant tribe by force, even though they were able on occasion to enlist the aid of tribes hostile to the one under attack, this aid was, at best, half-hearted. In 1737, after an indecisive war with the Fox Nation, Governor-general Beauharnois reported to the minister of marine that the Indian nations had their policies, just as the French had theirs, and they were not willing to see one of their nations (even a hostile one) destroyed, fearing that they might be next. "The Indians in general," Beauharnois wrote, "greatly fear us but they love us not at all and the attitudes they display to us are never sincere."[51] In short, the Indians regarded the French as just another nation, akin to themselves—more powerful in many ways, hence tolerated, but made to serve Indian aims whenever possible.

The west was the land of the Indians—indeed fur traders were obliged to travel in convoy. One or two canoes traveling alone were all too likely to be ambushed at a portage, the voyageurs killed and their trade goods or furs pillaged. Governors-general frequently complained of the heavy loss of life resulting from voyageurs, growing careless or impatient, who set off in small groups and were never heard of again.[52] A dispute in an Indian village was all too frequently settled by a swift blow from a tomahawk. When the French authorities discovered the identities of those responsible for such acts, and demanded retribution, they could expect to receive it only if the perpretrators' fellow tribesmen agreed. Every voyageur traveling to the Indian country was required by law to take a musket for self-defense and to return with it, on pain of a fine of three-hundred *livres*—two years' earnings. Many Canadians were killed when the tribe they happened to be with was attacked by an enemy tribe; here, too, the French could do nothing. On occasion they were taunted by the Indians for their failure to exact vengeance.[53]

Ironically, although the French sought by every means to keep the tribes in the west at peace with each other, it was only constant war among them that permitted the French to retain the upper hand.[54] At least twice the western tribes became so disgruntled with the French (likely owing to the scarcity and high prices of trade goods caused by the English wartime blockade of the Atlantic shipping lanes), and were so spurred on by the English authorities in New York, that several nations joined forces to drive the French out. The 1744 uprising proved abortive, but that of 1747 caused heavy casualties among the Canadians and required a determined military effort to suppress.[55] Had the English of New York had the wit to provide adequate support and stimulus, the French might well have lost complete control of the situation.

Despite such contretemps the French for over half a century enjoyed success in their policy of containing the westward drive of the English colonies. This was a result, to a considerable degree, of the ineptitude and racist attitude of the English colonials in their dealings with the Indians. From the very beginning of English settlement in Virginia and New England the Indians were regarded as little better than savage beasts who had to be driven out or destroyed to make way for godly English settlers.[56] In the eighteenth century a main factor that kept the Indians in the French alliance was the English fur traders' pernicious methods. In 1716 the Indian commissioners at Albany received a deputation from the Oneidas who complained of the dearness of goods and went on to state that many of the "far Indians" would come to Albany to trade but for the fact "that many of them have made the experiment, they found themselves so Scandalously imposed on and Cheated by the Traders that it discouraged them from returning."[57]

In contrast to this way of dealing, the French, for political more than economic reasons, went to great lengths to gain and hold the allegiance of the Indian nations. Every year over twenty thousand *livres* was budgeted for presents to be distributed to the various tribes. In some years, as in 1741, the sum rose to over sixty-five thousand *livres*, and in time of war the amounts spent to subsidize the Indian allies became astronomical.[58] The Indians, it might be noted, regarded these gifts not as presents but as tribute. Silver and enameled medallions were distributed to chiefs who had demonstrated their support of the French cause. When they went to Montreal to confer with the governor-general, they were wined and dined as would have been the ambassadors of European powers.[59] Some, to their great delight, had their portraits painted, and some were taken as honored guests on trips to Versailles to be impressed with the might and splendor of their French allies. When political pressure demanded it, the prices French traders offered for furs were raised by decree, and the post commanders were ordered to see to it that traders complied.[60] It was, therefore, no accident that the French garnered the lion's share of the fur trade.[61] The *American Gazetteer*, published in London in 1762, in the entry on Montreal commented, "The French have found some secret of conciliating the affections of the savages, which our traders seem stranger to, or at least take no care to put it in practice." Several of the French post commanders in the west might well have shaken their heads wryly had they read that observation. Yet the fact remains that when war came between England and France in America, the great majority of the Indian nations actively supported the French cause.

From 1700 on, French policy was to use Canada, Cape Breton, and Louisiana as pieces on the political and military chessboard to keep England and her colonies in check. Expansion of the English colonies had to be curbed. The population of the French colonies compared to that of the English was too meager to perform this task alone. Military assistance by the Indian nations was therefore vital. Distance, too, was vital for logistical reasons. In time of war, space could be traded for time. This required that the French first control that space, and that control could be maintained only with the concurrence of the peoples who occupied and dominated the space: the Indians.

In 1754 hostilities began in the Ohio Valley in a war—named the Seven Years' War by European historians, the French and Indian War by Americans, and the War of the Conquest by Canadians—that was to last to 1763. In North America, throughout this war, the policy of the French government was simple: use New France as a cat's paw. Keep the English on the defensive and oblige them to dispatch as large a proportion of their navy and army as possible to America. Keep them occupied there, hence unable to operate in Europe or against such vital parts of the French commercial empire as the West Indies, India, or the African slave coast. In this aim the French succeeded admirably, but still they lost the war.

Britain had to send over 23,000 regular troops of its 140,000-man army and a quarter of the Royal Navy to defend its colonies, in addition to raising some 22,000 colonial troops and militia. The French opposed this force with 12 of their 395 army infantry battalions, approximately 6,000 officers and men, plus 2,000 colonial regulars, the Canadian militia, and the Indian allies. The cost of the war is equally revealing. England spent eighty million pounds on the conquest of Canada; the total of the Canadian budgets for both civil and military purposes during the war years 1755–60 was less than five million pounds sterling.[62] Even at that, England succeeded in conquering Canada only as a result of the stupidity of the French commander, the marquis de Montcalm, and the incompetence of the Ministry of Marine.

The astonishing success the French military enjoyed in this war was largely a result of the strategy employed by the governor-general and commander-in-chief in New France, Pierre de Rigaud de Vaudreuil-Cavagnial. He was Canadian-born; in his youth he had voyaged through the west as a junior officer in the colonial regulars, and he subsequently rose to be governor of Louisiana. He understood the frontier in all its aspects and made excellent use of all that it had to offer. His strategy was to use the river routes that the French controlled, as well as the Indian allies. War parties of Indians, accompanied by Canadian militia and led by cadets of the regulars, ravaged the American frontier forts and settlements, tying down considerable forces for their defence. With the British and American forces dispersed all around the periphery of New France from Halifax to Albany to the Ohio, Vaudreuil was able to utilize his main force to strike swiftly before the enemy could muster superior numbers. In 1756, Oswego, the American fort and supply base on Lake Ontario, was taken and destroyed, giving the French control of the Great Lakes. The following year, while the main British force was being mustered at Halifax for an attack on Louisbourg, Vaudreuil launched an attack on Fort William Henry on Lake George, destroying it, and he would have gone on to destroy Fort Edward on the Hudson but for the pusillanimity of his field commander, Montcalm. Yet he at least had gained control of Lake Champlain, thereby blocking that invasion route to Canada. It was then Albany, not Montreal, that was threatened.

In all of these operations the Canadian militia and Indian auxiliaries played a prominent role. The Canadians, with their years of wilderness experience with the fur brigades, could travel and fight as well as or better than the Indians. They moved swiftly and silently along the rivers and through the forest, without baggage, living off the land; struck without warning; then faded back into the wilderness with their prisoners, scalps, and booty before the Anglo-American forces could react effectively. Despite the best efforts of the Canadians to curb the cruelty of the Indians and to protect their prisoners, many of the latter were killed, and some were savagely tortured. When an Indian war party, after a successful raid, ran out of food, it was not unusual for a prisoner to go into the cooking pot. Making one's food supply walk had definite military advantages. Such actions served as a form of psychological warfare. The Anglo-American forces, and the British regulars who had never encountered anything like it, were horrified and terrified. One sudden war whoop near a frontier fort or a supply convoy in the forest could cause immediate panic.

Despite the manifest success of Vaudreuil's extended frontier strategy and his guerrilla tactics, he was not without his critics. Montcalm, the obtuse, defeatist commander of the French army battalions, vociferously opposed both. Montcalm advocated the abandonment of the distant outposts and the recalling of all the colony's forces to the central colony in order to concentrate them for the invasion that was sure to come. Vaudreuil refused to order such action, declaring that with a virtual handful of men on the frontier, he tied down vastly superior enemy forces. He was well aware, given the size of the reinforcements sent from Britain, that eventually the forts in the west would have to be abandoned, but he intended to delay the event as long as possible, disputing the ground as he withdrew his forces. The farther he kept the enemy from the central colony, from Montreal and Quebec, the better. Once the enemy arrived there in force, the fate of the French empire in America could all too easily be settled in one brief battle, as proved to be the case. Vaudreuil relied on the fact that the war could not last forever; thus he persisted in his Fabian strategy of trading space for time, hoping that peace would come in Europe before he had exhausted both.

Without the support of the Indian allies, this strategy would have been out of the question. Their reasons for participating in the war so actively can only be guessed at. Some tribes from the far northwest appear to have joined in because they received ample supplies of goods before taking part in a campaign and were richly rewarded for the scalps and prisoners they brought in. For them it was more rewarding to hunt British soldiers and settlers than beaver. Another motive for supporting the French was that, down to 1758, they were the winning side. Those nations whose lands bordered on the advancing frontiers of Virginia and Pennsylvania clearly were taking advantage of the Anglo-French war to halt that advance. They were not so much allies of the French as the French were their allies, aiding them in their struggle for survival.

In this epic contest on the western frontier of European civilization from the viewpoint of the Indians waging war on their own eastern or southern frontiers, two things stand clear: first, none of the Indians appear to have envisaged the conquest of New France and the removal of French power from the continent; second, the Indians engaged in the war as independent, sovereign entities. They fought alongside the French and heeded their directives only when it suited them. As Montcalm's aide-de-camp, Louis-Antoine de Bougainville, remarked, "The Indians treat us imperiously, they lay down laws to us which they do not abide by themselves."[63] That these Indians allies consulted no interests but their own was made plain in 1758 when the Delawares, Shawnees, and Mingoes made their peace with the Anglo-Americans at Easton, Pennsylvania, in return for hollow assurances that lands taken from them would be returned.[64] That event marked the turning of the tide of war against the French. They were forced to abandon the Ohio Valley to the British.

In 1759, Montcalm threw away a glorious opportunity to destroy completely Wolfe's army at Quebec, and the city fell to the British.[65] The following year, owing to the ineptitude of the French Ministry of Marine, which failed to send reinforcements and supplies in time to its army besieging Quebec, the French forces were obliged to lay down their arms and surrender the colony. The French government, for long-range political reasons, then decided it would be best if Britain retained Canada at the end of the war. The colony and the Canadians were abandoned to their conquerors. Louisiana, again for political reasons, was ceded to Spain.[66]

In the terms of the Capitulation of Montreal, drafted by Vaudreuil, he (to his honor) inserted a clause: "The Savages or Indian
allies of his most Christian Majesty, shall be maintained in the Lands
they inhabit; if they choose to remain there; they shall not be mo-
lested on any pretence whatsoever, for having carried arms, and
served his most Christian Majesty. . . ."[67] The article was acceded
to by the British commander-in-chief, Jeffrey Amherst, and the
subsequent Proclamation of 1763 sought to enforce it. Yet with the
removal of French power in North America, the Indians were
doomed. They could no longer play the French off against the English and so retain their independence. When, outraged by the
treatment they received from the Anglo-American traders who took
over the old French posts, they attempted to drive those traders
and the British military out of the country, they were quickly
crushed.[68] There had been only one source of arms and supplies:
the very traders they sought to drive out. Once their limited stock
of arms and ammunition was exhausted, they had to submit.

In the Treaty of Paris, 1763, by articles four and seven, France
ceded "Canada and all its dependencies," including all the lands
east and north of the Mississippi with the exception of the city of
New Orleans.[69] No mention was made of the Indian nations whose
lands these were, nor, conveniently, was the validity of French claims
to sovereignty over those lands ever questioned. The Proclamation
of 1763 sought to protect the Indian nations temporarily from the
rapacity of land speculators and settlers, but it was clear that they
would be allowed to occupy their lands and continue their old way
of life only as long as the British government saw fit.

In the north, the fur trade frontier quickly revived with peace
and was pushed to its extreme limits, the Pacific and Arctic oceans.
Commercial rivalry between savagely competing fur trade companies, bringing in its train the unbridled sale of liquor to the Indians
(on whom it reacted as a toxic poison) followed by epidemics of
smallpox, reduced the northern and western tribes.[70] They were
thus unable to offer any resistance to the flood of settlers onto their
ancestral lands. The sad, demoralized remnants of these once proud
peoples were then herded onto reservations by the Canadian authorities with the expectation that the last of them would soon die
off and cease to be a problem. The old, unique frontier of New

France, a line having length but no breadth, was now replaced by the broad Turnerian frontier line of settlement. In Canada the coming of that new frontier had, inadvertently, been delayed by the French for two and one-half centuries.

NOTES

1. F. J. Turner, "The Rise and Fall of New France," *Minnesota History*, XVIII (December, 1937).

2. A. L. Burt, "The Frontier in the History of New France," *Canadian Historical Association Report, 1940*.

3. On this point Richard Pares commented, "The most important thing in the history of an empire is the history of its mother country. Colonial history is made at home" (cited in Dale Miquelon, *Dugard of Rouen* [Montreal, 1978], p. x). Walter Prescott Webb would not have been in agreement. In his *The Great Frontier* (Boston, 1952), p. 13, he states, "The overriding influence of the frontier on the Metropolis, on Western civilization, is of such importance as to require special emphasis." Such assertions he was able to make because he never really defined what he meant by the term *frontier*; usually he appears to mean the entire continent. This is clearly what is inferred by his statement (p. 13). "It was inherently a vast body of wealth without proprietors."

4. The best study to date of this early period is Marcel Trudel, *Histoire de la Nouvelle-France*, vol. I, *Les vaines tentatives, 1524–1603* (Montreal, 1963). On the destruction of the Saint Lawrence Iroquois, see J. V. Wright, *Quebec Prehistory* (Toronto, 1979), pp. 64–75.

5. Bruce Trigger, *The Children of Aataentsic*, 2 vols. (Montreal, 1976) II: 270, 327.

6. On French relations with the Hurons, see ibid.

7. Sherburne F. Cook and Woodrow Borah, *On the Credibility of Contemporary Testimony on the Population of Mexico in the Sixteenth Century*, Reprint No. 312 (Berkeley: Center for Latin American Studies, University of California).

8. E. E. Rich, *The History of the Hudson's Bay Company, 1770–1870* (London, 1958) I:610–13.

9. R. Glover, "The Difficulties of the Hudson's Bay Company's Penetration of the West," *Canadian Historical Review*, XXIX (September, 1948): 240–54.

10. R. Cole Harris and John Warkentin, *Canada before Confederation* (Toronto, 1974), pp. 32–46.

11. Jean, Evêque de Québec, to the minister, Québec, Sept. 10, 1726, Archives Nationales, Paris, Colonies (hereafter referred to as AN C11A), vol. 48, f. 434; M. le Coadjuteur de Québec, Oct. 15, 1729, ibid., vol. 51, f. 400; Montcalm to the minister, Montréal, Nov. 3, 1756, Service historique de l'Armée, Vincennes, A1, No. 294.

12. Fernand Braudel and Ernest Labrousse, eds., *Histoire économique et sociale de la France* (Paris, 1970) II:89, 529–52, 598–99, 672–78.

13. Richard Colebrook Harris, *The Seigneurial System in Early Canada* (Madison, Wis., 1966), pp. 71–73.

14. Trigger, *Children of Aataentsic*, II; J. H. Kennedy, *Jesuit and Savage in New France* (New Haven, 1950).

15. *Edits, ordonnances royaux, déclarations et arrêts du Conseil d'Etat du Roi concernant le Canada* (Québec, 1854), pp. 5–17.

16. Ibid., pp. 20–26.

17. Trigger, *Children of Aataentsic*, II.

18. W. J. Eccles, *The Canadian Frontier, 1534–1760* (Albuquerque, 1969), pp. 90–92.

19. Trigger, *Children of Aataentsic*, I:367–68.

20. Assemblies were occasionally called by the civil authorities to discuss specific issues, and edicts were subsequently promulgated by the royal officials to deal with them. See Allana G. Reid, "Representative Assemblies in New France," *Canadian Historical Review*, XXIII (March, 1946). There was, in fact, far more actual democracy in both old and New France than Webb imagined. A problem here is that he confused democracy with egalitarianism and liberty. See *The Great Frontier*, pp. 30–48.

21. Fernand Ouellet, "Propriété seigneuriale et groupes sociaux dans la vallée du Saint Laurent, 1660–1840," in *Mélanges d'histoire du Canada français offerts au professeur Marcel Trudel* (Ottawa, 1977), pp. 183–213.

22. Lucien Febvre, *Pour une Histoire à part entière* (Paris, 1962), pp. 481–528; Claude-Joseph de Ferrière, *Dictionnaire du droit* (Toulouse, 1779) II:329.

23. Pierre-François-Xavier de Charlevoix, S.J., *Histoire et description générale de la Nouvelle France, avec le journal historique d'un voyage fait par ordre du Roi dans L'Amérique septentrionale*, 3 vols. (Paris, 1744) III:272.

24. Etienne de Carheil, S.J., to Champigny, Michilimackinac, Aug. 30, 1702, in R. G. Thwaites, ed., *The Jesuit Relations and Allied Documents*, 73 vols. (Cleveland, 1896–1901), Fr. J-F. St. Cosme, Michilimackinac, Sept. 13, 1689, in *Rapport de l'Archiviste de la Province de Québec*, 1965 (hereafter referred to as *RAPQ*), p. 37.

25. Memoire instructif des intentions de Sa Majesté pour le Gouverneur et l'Intendant de Canada, 1716, AN C11A, vol. 36, f. 44; W. J. Eccles, *Frontenac the Courtier Governor* (Toronto, 1959), pp. 77–78.

26. Eccles, *Frontenac*, pp. 75–98.

27. Hubert Charbonneau and Yolande Lavoie, "Etude critique des sources de la période 1665–1668," *Revue de l'Histoire de l'Amérique française*, XXIV, no. 4 (March, 1971): 485–511.

28. Trigger, *Children of Aataentsic*, I:367–68.

29. Eccles, *Frontenac*, pp. 75–98, 273–93.

30. Ibid., pp. 90–91.

31. For an explanation of the problems attendant on the *congé* system and the leasing of the western posts, see La Galissonière to the minister, Québec, Oct. 23, 1748, AN C11A, vol. 91, ff. 231–34. A photograph of a *congé* issued to the Sieur de la Vérendrye appears in *RAPQ*, 1922–23, facing p. 228.

32. The bulk of these *engagements* are conserved at the Archives Nationales du Québec à Montréal.

33. Here again conditions on the Canadian frontier bear no resemblance to those that Webb described as bound to prevail on the North American frontier. See *The Great Frontier*, pp. 30–45.

34. St. Pierre to Beauharnois, Poste des Miamis, 1741, Archives du Séminaire

68 W. J. ECCLES

de Québec, Fonds Verreau, Carton 5, No. 5; Beauharnois to St. Pierre, Montréal, July 22, 1742, ibid., No. 13; La Galissonière to M. de St. Pierre, commandant à Missilimakinac, Québec, Sept. 4, 1748, ibid., no. 53.

35. In startling contrast here is the eighteenth-century Carolina frontier, where the settlers are depicted by one educated observer as sunk deeper in barbarism than the Indians. See Richard J. Hooker, *The Carolina Backcountry on the Eve of the Revolution* (Williamsburg, Va., 1955).

36. Eccles, *Frontenac*, pp. 273–94.

37. Mémoire sur les postes du Canada adressé à M. de Surlaville en 1754 par M. le Chevalier de Raymond, *RAPQ*, 1927–28, p. 334; Fernand Ouellet, "Dualité économique et changement technologique au Québec (1760–1790)," *Histoire Sociale, Social History*, IX, no. 18 (November, 1976): 260–61.

38. W. J. Eccles, "The Social, Economic, and Political Significance of the Military Establishment in New France," *Canadian Historical Review*, LII, no. 1 (March, 1971): 1–22.

39. Guy Frégault, "La Compagnie de la Colonie," *Revue de l'Université d'Ottawa*, January–March, 1960, pp. 5–29; April–June, 1960, pp. 127–49.

40. Eccles, *Frontenac*, pp. 285–94.

41. W. J. Eccles, *France in America* (New York, 1972), pp. 102–103.

42. Vaudreuil, Beauharnois, Raudot to the minister, Québec, Oct. 19, 1705, *RAPQ*, 1938–39, p. 99; Hocquart to the minister, Québec, Oct. 25, 1729, AN C11A, vol. 51, f. 264.

43. E. B. O'Callaghan and J. R. Brodhead, eds., *Documents Relating to the Colonial History of New York*, 15 vols. (Albany, 1856–1883), X:269.

44. "Mémoire du Roy à MM de Vaudreuil et Bégon," May 30, 1724, in *Nouvelle-France: Documents historiques: Correspondance échangée entre les autorités françaises et les gouverneurs et intendants* (Québec, 1893), I:58; Max Savelle, *The Diplomatic History of the Canadian Boundary 1749–1763* (New Haven, 1940), pp. 7–8.

45. Vaudreuil to the minister, Montréal, April 3, 1704, *RAPQ*, 1938–39, p. 25. This removal of the Abenakis occasioned a bitter protest from Marguerite Hertel, widow of the seigneur of Saint-François, a part of whose seigneury was appropriated for the Indians. Her protest was rejected by the Crown. The incident marks what was perhaps the only occasion on which lands were taken from European title holders for the benefit of Indians. See Marguerite Hertel, veuve Crevier, to M. de Beauharnois, intendant, Saint-François, Jan. 23, 1703, Public Archives of Canada, Beauharnois Papers (M.G. 18, G6); Le Conseil de Marine, Jan. 19, 1722, in *Nouvelle-France: Documents historiques*, I:187–88.

46. The map of the western part of New France by M. Bellin, Ingénieur du Roy et de la Marine, published in 1755, indicates various areas as *Pays des*, "the country of," the different nations. The regions north of Lakes Huron and Superior are marked, "Toute cette coste n'est pas connue. On ne connoit point le cours de toutes ces Rivières [This entire area is unknown. No one knows the course of all these rivers]." Specific rivers are marked *Rivière Inconnue à tous les géographes*.

47. But see W. P. Webb, *Great Frontier*, p. 3, where the Indians are dismissed as being of no consequence in the history of the frontier. Their lands are treated as vacant and the very existence of the Indians is barely acknowledged. He wrote: "I am ignoring the scattered Indian population who did present some resistance but were not a major problem except for the few people who were in contact with them

on the farthest fringes of settlement." Here again, Webb's peculiar notion of what constituted the frontier raises serious questions.

48. Memoire pour servir d'instruction au Sr Le Gardeur de St. Pierre . . . commandant aux Forts la Reine, Dauphin, Maurepass . . . , La Jonquiere, Montréal, May 27, 1750, Archives du Séminaire de Québec, Fonds Verreau, Carton 5, No. 33.

49. Memoire ou Extrait du Journal Sommaire du Voyage de Jacques Le gardeur . . . Sr de St. Pierre . . . chargé de la Decouverte de la Mer de Louest, ibid., No. 54.

50. Ibid.

51. Beauharnois to the minister, Québec, Oct. 17, 1736, AN C11A, vol. 65, f. 143.

52. A. S. Morton, *A History of the Canadian West to 1870–71* (London, 1939), pp. 252–53; Fernand Grenier, ed., *Papiers Contrecoeur et autres documents concernant le conflit anglo-français sur l'Ohio de 1745 à 1756* (Quebec, 1952), p. 193; Vaudreuil to Beauharnois, Nouvelle Orléans, Nov. 9, 1745, Loudon Collection, Huntington Library.

53. Journal de Marin fils, *RAPQ*, 1963, vol. 41, pp. 251–55.

54. D'Aigremont to the minister, Québec, Nov. 14, 1708, AN C11A, vol. 29, f. 44.

55. Journal de M. Bougainville, *RAPQ*, 1923–24, p. 273; Eccles, *Canadian Frontier*, pp. 151–54.

56. Alden T. Vaughan, "'Expulsion of the Salvages': English Policy and the Virginia Massacre of 1622," *William and Mary Quarterly*, 3rd ser., XXXV, no. 1 (January, 1978): 57–84; Francis Jennings, *The Invasion of America: Indians, Colonialism, and the Cant of Conquest* (Chapel Hill, N.C., 1975).

57. Peter Wraxall, *An Abridgement of the New York Indian Records*, ed. C. H. McIlwain (Cambridge, Mass., 1915), p. 111.

58. Hocquart to the minister, Québec, Oct. 24, 1741, AN C11A, vol. 76, ff. 14–15. For a detailed but rather partisan treatment of this subject, see W. R. Jacobs, *Indian Diplomacy and Indian Gifts: Anglo-French Rivalry along the Ohio and Northwest Frontier, 1748–1763* (Stanford, 1950).

59. For the impression such treatment made on one Onondaga chieftain, see the entry of Teganissorens in *The Dictionary of Canadian Biography* (Toronto, 1969), II:619–23.

60. Fernand Grenier, ed. *Papiers Contrecoeur* pp. 264–65.

61. Murray G. Lawson, *Fur: A Study in English Mercantilism, 1700–1775* (Toronto, 1943).

62. Guy Frégault, *La guerre de la conquête* (Montreal, 1955), p. 283. The English translation of this work, entitled *Canada: The War of the Conquest* (Toronto, 1969), p. 203, mistranslates these figures grievously; £80 millions given as the cost to Britain of the conquest of Canada in the original French edition is rendered as £4 millions.

63. Journal de M. Bougainville, *RAPQ*, 1923–24, p. 227.

64. Douglas Edward Leach, *The Northern Colonial Frontier, 1607–1763* (New York, 1966), p. 203.

65. W. J. Eccles, "The Battle of Quebec: A Reappraisal," *Proceedings of the Third Annual Meeting, the French Colonial Historical Society, 1978* (Athens, Ga., 1978).

66. W. J. Eccles, "The Role of the American Colonies in Eighteenth-Century French Foreign Policy," in *Atti del I Congresso Internazionale di Storia Americana* (Genoa, 1976), pp. 163–73.

67. Adam Shortt and Arthur G. Doughty, *Documents Relating to the Constitutional History of Canada, 1759–1791* (Ottawa, 1918), I:33.

68. Francis Parkman, *The Conspiracy of Pontiac* (Boston, 1851); Howard H. Peckham, *Pontiac and the Indian Uprising* (Chicago, 1947). It must be said that the above-mentioned dated works are both highly unsatisfactory treatments of this important episode. A critical examination, viewing it from both sides of the hill and not just from that of the Anglo-Americans, is long overdue.

69. Zenab Esmat Rashed, *The Peace of Paris, 1763* (Liverpool, 1951), pp. 216–18.

70. Arthur S. Morton, *A History of the Canadian West to 1870–71* (Toronto, 1939), pp. 329–33.

WARREN DEAN

Ecological and Economic Relationships in Frontier History: São Paulo, Brazil

THE Brazilian frontier known as the Paulista West is an area of some two hundred thousand square kilometers in the interior of the state of São Paulo. This region maintained an internal demarcation between white and aboriginal settlement for three and one-half centuries. The first whites appeared on the edge of the frontier in the 1550s, and the last native American tribal lands were appropriated only after 1900. It was a nearly static frontier for a very long time. Until the beginning of sugar and coffee planting in the nineteenth century, it contained only a very sparse human population, but from the 1870s onward, when Brazil's coffee began to find an increasing overseas market, the inrush of native whites, accompanied at first by slaves and then by some two million European immigrants, erased in a few years the entire primeval landscape and replaced it with coffee groves, subsistence crops, and pastures.[1]

In the comparative history of the world economy of the nineteenth and twentieth centuries, this was an important frontier. It will be examined here mostly from an ecological point of view. Other themes—institutional transformation, the role of government, and the treatment of native populations—will be considered here in relation to the theme of ecological degradation, which the settlement of the area exemplifies. The importance of this subject is evident, even though it is difficult to study the relationship retrospectively. The principal problem is that contemporaneous sources, mostly the written reports of whites, were negligent in observing ecological phenomena. For the most part, the writers were ignorant of those phenomena and were thoroughly subjective, even perverse, in their view of human activities in the natural environment—especially because it was a frontier—as beneficial and even divinely ordained.

The Natural Environment

The environment encountered by the first Europeans was not a
hostile one, even though it must have looked extremely strange to
them. The coast of São Paulo, hemmed in by a crystalline escarpment eight hundred meters high, was covered with tropical rain
forest. Patches of that forest are still in place, relatively untouched.
Once that barrier was overcome, however, the whites entered a
new environment. Altitude moderates the climate. Temperatures
in the Paulista West average 22° C in January and 6–10° C daily in
the coldest winter month of July. Temperatures below 0° C are normally not experienced in the extreme northwest of the state, and
only one or two days a year in the remainder of the region. Rainfall,
very heavy along the coastal range, is 1,250 mm annually in most
of the region, rising to 1,500 mm along the eastern border with
Minas Gerais. Rainfall becomes more seasonal from south to north;
in the south there is a barely perceptible seasonality, while in the
north it extends up to four months during the winter. Seasonality is
not as extreme as yearly variation, which surpasses 25 percent in
some parts of the interior.[2]

The Paulista West is part of the immense watershed of the Paraná River, which joins the Paraguay and finally empties into the
Río de la Plata. In the state of São Paulo this watershed extends all
the way to the coastal range. The Paulista West may therefore be
considered a vast inclined plane, drained by parallel northwest-
flowing tributaries. The underlying structure is basalt and gneiss.
Cutting across this plane is a low basaltic outcropping, dividing the
region into two areas: the Western Plateau and the Peripheral
Depression. Both have been subject to a series of complex sedi-
mentary processes since the Mesozoic era.

The soils of the Paulista West are derived largely from basalt
and sandstone, which have weathered mainly through chemical
processes. The basaltic soils are rich in iron, which imparts a dark
reddish brown color, and in calcium, manganese, and aluminum.
The humus of the forest cover maintained the porosity of these soils,
despite their high clay content, and their great depth made them
extremely water-retentive. The sandstone-derived soils, inter-
spersed among the basaltic but more generally distributed closer to

GOIAS

MINAS GERAIS

○ Uberoba

S. Ana do ○ R. Grande
Parnaiba ○
Itapura ○
Western Plateau R. Tietê Falls ×Avanhandava
MATO GROSSO DO SUL R. Aguapei
R. Pardo R. do Peixe
R. Parana
R. Paranapanema Campos ○ Novos
Tropic of Capricorn
PARANA
△ △

R. Pardo
Franca ○
Casa Branca
○ Araraquara
Rio Claro ○ ○ Mogi-
Piracicaba ○ Mirim
○ Campinas
Botucato ○ Porto ○ Jundiai
Sorocaba ○ ○Feliz
△ São Paulo ○
△ Peripheral Depression △ △
△ Coastal Range Santos ○

Atlantic Ocean

△

50 Km 0   50   100 150 Km

.... ROUTES
△ ALDEAMENTOS
○ TOWNS

State of São Paulo, Brazil: Paulista West in the Eighteenth Century

the Paraná River, vary in calcium content; those which are poorer in calcium are more easily eroded. Thus, the drainage system has left in place at the higher elevations soils which are more fertile because they are less acid.[3]

Native vegetation of the Paulista West has been divided into three types: tropical semideciduous forest; *campos* ("fields," that is, grasslands); and *campos cerrados* (closed fields), more loosely called *cerrados*. The last type has an appearance intermediate between the other two. Gradations locally recognized between *cerrado* and *campo* are *campo sujo* ("dirty field"), and *cerrado* and forest, called *cerradão*.

The *cerrado* presents only two trophic levels: herbaceous, with a predominance of Gramineae and Cyperaceae, and an upper level of stunted trees or bushes, among which may be mentioned *barbatimão (Stryphnodendron barbatimao), pau-santo (Kielmeyera coriacea), pequi (Caryocar brasiliensis)*, and *pau-terra (Qualea* spp.). The *cerrado* is associated with a drier climate than is the forest, since its species have adapted to a seasonal lack of moisture in the upper meter or two of soil. It does not exhibit true xeromorphism, since the species located there have not had to adapt techniques of water conservation or storage because ground water is available throughout the year.[4]

Primary forests of the Paulista West have all been eliminated except for very small patches from their original state, largely tropical, in which semideciduous and nondeciduous arboreal species mingled. Periodicity of the foliage marked the dry and wet seasons. Among the dominants were *peroba (Aspidosperma* spp.), *cedro (Cedrela* spp.), *canela (Nectandra* spp.), *jatobá (Hymenaea* spp.), and *paineira (Chorisia* spp.). These trees formed an upper canopy thirty meters high, under which could be found a second arboreal and at least two subarboreal levels with sufficient access to sunlight to include heliotrophs. Those areas enjoying more rainfall were bountifully endowed with epiphytes and lianas. Mixed with the dominants in the southern part of the state, at higher, cooler elevations, were araucaria pines (*Araucaria angustifolia*), which formed immense stands across the Paranapanema River in the state of Paraná.[5]

The *campo* is the most difficult of the three types to reconstruct historically because it was the easiest to transform. Travelers at the beginning of the nineteenth century mention in passing an absence of bushes and the dominance of grasses, including *barba-de-bode* (*Aristida* spp.) and *capim-flexa* (*Trystachya leistachya*), which grew to a height of no more than half a meter.

Appropriation of the original standing resources of the frontier may be said to constitute the frontier's essential history. The concept of a "windfall," advanced by Professor Webb, expresses this view. It must be determined, therefore, what the extent of that stock of resources, may have been. The problem is difficult in relation to the Paulista West because it was a zone of transition in which all three types of vegetation reached their farthest extent. It is not possible, at present, to state which types, in historical times, were in advance and which in retreat. By 1800, observations of distribution were made in limited areas of the interior. By that time, however, much human intervention may have taken place, so even these sparse notices cannot be taken as firm evidence of the original distribution.

The problem has been examined by ecologists and geographers mainly in relation to a definition of the *cerrado*.[6] It has been found that some three hundred species are exclusive to the *cerrado*, although they do not display adaptations suggesting a long period of evolution. Many of these species have low nutrient requirements and are tolerant of ionized aluminum, which is present in *cerrado* soils. An enormous area of Brazil, from Maranhão in the north to Mato Grosso do Sul in the south—a quarter of the land surface—is covered by *cerrado*. This area therefore may represent a true climax, distinct from *campo* or forest, showing the adaptation of a community to soils which are poorer than those invaded by forest, served by scarcer and more seasonal rain but more retentive of water than those covered by *campo*. The *cerrado* would tend to invade *campo* in periods of greater rainfall and would invade forest in drier periods, assisted by lightning-kindled fire, which is common and may occur even in rain forest.

It is also possible that *cerrado* is merely a successional stage, invading *campo* as groundwater becomes increasingly fixed by grasses and improving the porosity of the soil through its own additions of decayed root systems. In this view, the forest, as true climax, would improve the soil further through its deposits of litter, which produce humus that the forest itself recycles. The forest would alter the microclimate as it spreads, reducing the seasonality of rain and moderating temperature extremes.

Finally, it is possible that the *cerrado* is a disclimax, caused by the impoverishment of soils through human action. The repeated setting of fires has the effect of degrading forest to *cerrado* and to *campo* quite independently of climate change. Although in their original state the soils of the Paulista West were among the world's richest, the removal of forest cover destroys their carrying capacity, since their fertility derives largely from the fragile layer of humus. In the absence of vegetation, rain leaches calcium, which increases acidity. Acids reduce aluminum, abundant in these soils, to an ionized state, in which condition it competes freely for nitrogen, phosphates, and other nutrients needed by the vegetation. Ionized aluminum is also directly toxic to most plants. Iron, which remains in the upper horizon, or somewhat below the surface, forms oxides which render the soil impermeable to rain, causing rapid erosion of the humus. The heat of the sun, in extreme cases, then bakes the dense iron oxides into bricklike laterite.

Empirical studies have given support to each of these theories concerning the *cerrado*. The capacity of each of the vegetational systems to maintain itself in anomalous conditions, however, makes it difficult to reach a conclusion regarding the nature of the *cerrado*. It has therefore been suggested that the *cerrado* at its center is a true climax, but that on its fringes, which would include São Paulo, it is a disclimax.[7]

The attribution of the *cerrado* to human intervention constitutes the second reason why the subject of original distribution is a historical problem. If humans have in fact intervened on the necessary scale, they may have left some record of those acts, or at least of their indirect effects. It seems likely that forest covered all of the Paulista West originally, with the exception of certain high tablelands west of the basalt outcroppings and near the border with Minas Gerais where drainage is too rapid to permit the invasion of arboreal or subarboreal species. If forest was absent anywhere else, it may have been along the lower river valleys farther from the rivercourses, where sediments were naturally eroded.

Before the European Invasion

Thus, the forest may have extended, before human intervention, over nearly the entire Paulista West. This is difficult to affirm, because human presence there is perhaps ten thousand years old, long enough to have intensified climatic and microclimatic changes. By that date the dwellers at Lagoa Santa, Minas Gerais, were probably using fire.[8] The result of their activity has not been evaluated, but burning of vegetation by hunterers-gathers may have taken place in all three of these ecosystems to drive prey, kill snakes, or lure prey by stimulating fresh growth of grasses.[9] Burning for any of these purposes may have spread accidentally.

With the appearance of semiagricultural tribes in the area about a thousand years ago, or five hundred years before the whites, burning can be confidently asserted. The tribes of the Paulista West were the Guarani, Tupiniquim, and Tupinambá. São Paulo was for these tribes also a frontier. The center of Guarani settlement was to the west and southwest. Pressing eastward by the time the Portuguese arrived, they maintained a major trail that crossed the state of Paraná and southern São Paulo and terminated near Santos. The Tupinambá arrived in São Paulo from the east, while the Tupiniquim occupied the region between.

All these groups were considerably dependent on farming for food calories. Principally they cultivated corn and root crops: *cassava, aipim, inhame,* and *cará (Dioscorea* spp.), *mangarito (Xanthosoma* spp.), and sweet potatoes. They also grew peanuts, pumpkins, and tobacco. Planting was done on forested land because of the fertility of its humus. The forest was cleared by cutting, to dry out the underbrush, followed by burning, which destroyed most of the trees and charred the rest. Burning turned the entire mass of vegetation and litter into minerals immediately available for absorption by the crops. At the same time it eliminated weed and insect competitors. The clearing was planted several years in succession. Each time, planting was preceded by burning. The field was finally abandoned when an appreciable decline in fertility set in.

This system of planting, called slash-and-burn, or swidden, is immensely wasteful of standing vegetation but is efficient in producing food calories with minimum labor. In areas where soil and climate are favorable, the forest will grow back to a stand of second growth in about thirty years. This forest, called *capoeira*, is easily distinguished from primary stands; it is lower, less dense, and less complex. Second growth was easier to cut and burn than primary, although primary was easier to plant, since a burned-over field of secondary forest was weed-infested.

The Tupi-Guarani cultivators could not expand to the point of occupying, and degrading, all the available forest, because they reached a crisis of protein supply earlier. These tribes did not domesticate animals for food—indeed this is nearly impossible in a swidden regime—but depended for protein on hunting and fishing, on gathering of *içá* (ant paste), and on nuts. Their plantings were left untended while they moved in yearly migrations to the coast to catch fish and shellfish and to the araucaria pine forests in Paraná to collect pine nuts to be smoked and stored.[10]

These activities imply a population sufficiently dense that agriculture was critical to its survival. Apparently the Tupi-Guarani were more intensive agriculturalists than were later tribal peoples in the area. Constant warfare among and between tribes may also be taken as a sign of competition for resources. It is possible that the native population in the Paulista West, over the five hundred years of agriculture before the Europeans, averaged one per square kilometer, that is, about two hundred thousand. Since each person would have required about one-tenth hectare per year of plantings, over five centuries, ten million hectares would have been burned. Burning would have occurred repeatedly in the same places. Supposing that ten burnings in the same field would under any conditions discourage further planting, then perhaps 5 percent of the Paulista West was thus transformed before the arrival of the whites.

Additional lands may have been degraded by burning to drive or lure game, or accidentally. Nevertheless, the total does not appear to have been substantial. Certainly it is not enough to account for the corridor of *cerrado* between Franca and Mogi-Mirim and for the *campos* of Araraquara, Avanhandava, and Rio Pardo–Campos Novos. Unless earlier burning by nonagricultural peoples is judged to have been more damaging, most of the open areas observed by the 1500s seem not to be attributable to the Indians.

It is interesting, however, that the Tupi language provides a word to describe erosion caused by groundwater flowing through soil that has lost its root system: *voçoroca*. It also supplies a word for one of the products of laterization, *tapanhoacanga*, though this is apparently a neologism. Both words may have been used by mestizo Tupi speakers after 1500. It is also significant that the French naturalist Saint-Hilaire was surprised to learn that the area around the city of São Paulo was *campo* in 1500, when at the time of his observation in 1819 it seemed appropriate for forest.[11]

The European Invasion

The Portuguese arrived at the coast of São Paulo in the 1530s. Their first activity, sugar planting, quickly lost its importance as plantations were begun farther north, in Bahia and Pernambuco, nearer the metropolitan market. The other principal trade good of the colony, brazilwood, a red dyestuff, did not extend as far south as São Paulo. The first contacts of the Portuguese with the Tupi-Guarani led to the enslavement of the Indians either for household labor or fieldwork on the coastal sugar plantations.

Constant warfare among tribal groups greatly facilitated the intrusion of whites on the plateau. The first white settlement, which became the permanent center of expansion and is today the center of the metropolis of São Paulo, was located on an elevation in the first *campo* the Portuguese found after surmounting the escarpment. They fortified it and began to raid for slaves, an activity which continued, with varying intensity, until the start of the nineteenth century. The Tupi-Guarani were highly susceptible to smallpox, measles, and lung infections; most of each levy brought to the town of São Paulo were fatally stricken, leading to the necessity of further raids.

Clearly, slave-raiding constituted a peculiar form of frontier expansion. The Europeans in this area did not barter with tribal peoples for goods derived from their traditional hunting and gathering complex. Animal pelts were not traded in the Paulista West, and forest products, such as vanilla, while not ignored, were of small commercial import. The coastal escarpment prevented a trade in lumber, which might have altered considerably the Europeans' initial relationship to the forest. São Paulo offered only one extractive product of value: its human forest dwellers. In spite of the vast expanse which had to be scoured, slaves presented the advantage of being a product that could be walked to market.

The colonists were somewhat embarrassed in their depredations by the Jesuit missionaries who accompanied them. Jesuits, interested only in conversion, opposed Indian slavery and managed to extract from the Crown repeated prohibitions. Colonists, nevertheless, relentlessly pressed upon the Tupi-Guarani. Those slaves they took to farm their own estates they called *administrados* (administered persons) under the pretext that they had received them from public authorities as wards. A few colonists numbered their retinues in the hundreds. Continual attacks upon the Indians caused some tribal groups to sue for peace. These groups were conducted to *aldeamentos*, or settlements, similar to the *reducción* in Spanish territories.[12] At first placed in the control of the Jesuits, these *aldeamentos* later were taken over by the governors. They were endowed with lands, but not sufficient to enable the tribal people to continue hunting and gathering, which the Jesuits condemned as idleness.[13]

Even under these conditions of cultural and physical degradation, Indians and Europeans exchanged techniques of environmental exploitation. From the beginning the Portuguese depended on the Tupi-Guarani for food supplies, including fish and game. The slaves continued to plant native domesticates. So accustomed did the colonists become to consuming maize that they came to call it *milho*, a generic word for meal (just as in American English it has become known by a generic word for grain). Colonists accepted the Indian practice of burning and planting in the forest. They did not attempt to teach their slaves to employ the European complex of plow farming. The additional labor which the plow required would have been in economic terms irrational; thin population implied extensive, not intensive cultivation. The Portuguese therefore continued, under more precarious conditions, the Indian custom of living off the natural accumulation of capital in the vegetation and soil.

The Portuguese brought to São Paulo and installed in the swidden complex a wide variety of domesticates, including wheat, beans, rice, sugar cane, and bananas. These not only were cultivated by subdued Indians but were also passed from tribe to tribe beyond the frontier. Colonists also brought chickens and swine. Chickens were difficult to raise outside the towns because they were defenseless against predators. Pigs, however, were hardy and could be left to root in the forest. In towns, fruit trees were planted—peaches, figs, oranges, and limes. The Portuguese introduction of iron knives, axes, and hoes permitted more intensive cultivation.[14]

Cattle raising was an enormous agricultural novelty and was adapted to the new environment in a manner quite different from production in Europe. Cattle were not integrated within the farming system but were set loose in open fields to roam and feed as they would. Again, the logic was to conserve labor and capital. Mild climate dispensed with the need to stable animals or to store forage. Besides the *campo* surrounding the city of São Paulo, more was available in patches in the direction of Sorocaba. It was estimated that forty to fifty-five head might graze on one square kilometer and that a herd of three thousand to four thousand might be managed by no more than six hands.

The mestizo agricultural system transformed the relationship of humans to the environment. The new staple crops, three of them Gramineae, were more demanding of the soil than any of the native domesticates, with the exception of corn. Beans, rice, and pigs increased the supply of protein, making possible the transformation of hunters-gatherers into a stable peasantry.

Population within the white-colonized area had risen to about two per square kilometer by 1600, and per-capita cropland had risen to about six-tenths hectare per person. São Paulo was perhaps the only town with a population over two hundred persons. The frontier by then extended along the coast as far south as Iguape, on the highland along the Paraíba do Sul River valley from Río de Janeiro to São Paulo, and in an arc about sixty kilometers in radius around the capital from Jundiaí to Itu to Sorocaba. Beyond this for several hundred kilometers slave hunting had eliminated the Indian population.

Exploration and Westward Expansion

A series of distant political events propelled the whites forward to immensely longer expeditions in the second quarter of the seventeenth century. The absorption of the Portuguese Crown by the king of Spain provided the colonists in Portuguese territory a pretext to cross the boundary drawn by the Treaty of Tordesillas. This line passed north to south through the Paulista West. Expeditions were sent to the region of Spanish Jesuit reductions in the western part of the present-day state of Paraná. The Guarani there were enslaved, and the Jesuits fled west and south. When the Portuguese succeeded in reestablishing their independence in 1640, Spanish territory became fair game. The Crown, with most of its Asian trading posts lost to the Dutch, now sought more intensive profit from its New World colony. The colonists of São Paulo were therefore set to hunt for mines of silver and gold.

Settlers had in fact kept an eye out for precious metals since their first days on the plateau. Small amounts of gold had indeed been found a few kilometers north and west of the capital.[15] Encouragement by the Crown now opened an area of three and one-half million square kilometers, including all the present states from Río Grande do Sul to Goias in the north, which were claimed to be part of the captaincy-general of São Paulo. The combined search for precious metals and slaves went on for fifty years.

This was the heroic epoch of the *bandeiras*, officially sanctioned expeditions, privately sponsored and equipped. As many as two or three thousand joined, remaining in the forest for several years, in penetrations that extended for two or three thousand kilometers or more. Their techniques were entirely indigenous since they went afoot, along forest trails beaten by the Indians, and engaged in itinerant hunting and planting, always doubling back to collect the harvest. The *bandeiras* have been elevated to a myth in which their slave-raiding mission is muted while their role in expanding Brazilian boundaries is triumphantly elaborated. And, at last, the *bandeiras* located immense deposits of gold, first in Minas Gerais, then in Mato Grosso and Goias, profoundly transforming the economy of the colony.[16]

The effect of the *bandeiras*, from the 1620s to the 1720s, was to complete the eradication of tribal peoples as far as the Paraná River. Those groups which were not subjugated had withdrawn further north, west, and south. The practice of slaving had worked a kind of triage upon the tribes: those least given to war and most agricultural had been captured or reduced. The survivors had evolved a culture modeled on the *bandeiras*, largely abandoning farming in favor of predation, living off stores accumulated by other tribes, and capturing them for slaves. Thus the Caiapó, who lived near the confluence of the Rio Grande and the Paraná, engaged in piracy as far as the mouth of the Tietê, and the Gualaxó, of Mato Grosso do Sul, acquired the horse from the Spanish and were more than a match for the still dismounted *bandeiras*. Periodic depopulation of São Paulo by the *bandeiras* and the predation upon the native population during the first two centuries of European conquest imply, in the Paulista West, a decline in the intensiveness of human attack upon the forest and its reestablishment in marginal areas beyond the white frontier.[17]

The *bandeiras*, shortly after the first discoveries of gold in Minas Gerais in 1695, suffered a terrible reverse. They were expelled from the region by newcomers from Bahia, who managed to obtain the political dismemberment of that region from São Paulo. Meanwhile, the Paulistas continued the search for gold and located two other alluvial fields in Mato Grosso, about fifteen hundred kilometers northwest of the city of São Paulo, and in Goiás, about one thousand kilometers north-northwest. Both these strikes were far beyond the areas cleared of Indians and were extremely difficult to reach.

The earliest form of communication with Cuiabá was by water. Dugout canoes were launched in the Tietê a few miles beyond Itu at a place now called Porto Feliz. These river convoys (expeditions of three thousand or more men), called *monções*, then followed the Paraná to the Rio Pardo, proceeding up that river and down others until Cuiabá was reached, a journey of more than two months. Monções continued throughout the eighteenth century, though less frequently after a road was opened in 1737 between São Paulo and Goiás and then extended to Cuiabá. The colonial government, however, remained interested in the river route because it more directly linked the coast with the boundaries it wished to defend in Mato Grosso, from Iguatemi to Bela Vista, Aquidauana, and Albuquerque.[18]

Canoe building represented the first intensive use of forest hardwoods. These vessels were fifteen to twenty meters long, and each convoy required about three hundred. The canoe makers preferred peroba wood and apparently succeeded in denuding the area of Porto Feliz. By 1760 a rise in the price of trunks led to canoes being launched far upriver. In the Paulista West the tallest trees were normally found along watercourses, yet later travelers mentioned a curious lack of them along the Tietê. It is likely that the building of dugouts eliminated trees over fifteen meters tall along the river as far as Avanhandava. The Tietê and Piracicaba apparently ran clear until historic times, with little transport of sediment, but with the felling of trees they became extremely turbid. It is possible that the *monções* ended because of the scarcity of perobas of acceptable size at convenient distances from the launching sites.[19]

It is more likely, however, that the expansion of horse and mule breeding made possible a shift that was in fact preferable. The gold fields of Minas Gerais were of such immense value that the other areas of Brazil were substantially reoriented toward supplying Minas Gerais with foodstuffs and animals. In the 1720s, therefore, Paulistas in great numbers began to take up ranching in the southern provinces of Rio Grande do Sul and Santa Catarina, dismembered from São Paulo in 1738, and in Paraná, which remained part of São Paulo until 1854.[20] There was the region of the Campos Gerais, the "fields everywhere," which reached their easternmost extension east of the city of São Paulo and gradually broadened as they spread into Paraná. The *campos* extended even further, beyond Rio Grande do Sul, where they merged with the Uruguayan and Argentine pampas.

Cattle, horses, and mules bred in the Campos Gerais were brought to the yearly fair at Sorocaba. By the early nineteenth century thirty thousand to forty thousand were sold annually. Most of the animals were driven onward to Minas Gerais, by way of Atibaia, or to the city of Río de Janeiro. Some mules were sold to drivers who made the immense journey to Goiás and Cuiabá.

A mule train was much more economical in use of labor power than the canoe convoy. Mules, however, were limited in utility because they could not traverse forest. Earlier penetrations of the Paulista West had followed the Indian routes, which were always forest trails. The Tupi-Guarani required forest, and so did the *bandeiras*, because they had sustained themselves with hunting and swidden cultivation. But mules required forage; mule trains had to follow grasslands, and the drivers had to be fed at settlements scattered along the forest margin.

The best route for passage to Goiás was along the eastern border with Minas Gerais, from Jundiaí to Mogi-Mirim to Casa Branca to Franca, then across the Río Grande to Uberaba and northward. Along this distance, except for brief interruptions, stretched a rather narrow band of *campo* and *cerrado* oriented north to south. The town of Franca was in the midst of a relatively large expanse of *campo* and therefore began to develop as a cattle-raising center. The *cerrado* along the Goiás road was the furthest extension west and south of the immense *cerrados* of Minas Gerais.

The Caipira *Frontier*

Establishment of overland trade with the mines and of cattle ranches opened the wayside to settlement by squatters. The frontier provided the attraction of more abundant harvests in primeval forest. But the settlement was not merely a reaction to relative fertility of the soil. Frontier people, or pioneers, in São Paulo were called *caipiras*, from a Tupi expression probably meaning "cutters of forest" or "forest cultivators." Their origin was in the racial blending of Indians, whites, and African freedmen, with the Indian stock predominating. They were thus also called *caboclos*, from a Tupi expression meaning "mestizo," applied as a pejorative. During the eighteenth century this subordinate social group came gradually to be perceived by the white dominant group as both racially somewhat distinct and culturally inferior.

Subordination of the *caipiras* consisted specifically of their exclusion from landownership. In theory the colonial authorities granted land to anyone who was willing to work it. The grants, or *sesmarias*, were bestowed, however, only upon the most prominent persons in a locality. Moreover, they were always for immense amounts of land—a square league, usually, or 43.56 square kilometers. The intention was to establish a landed aristocracy which would be loyal to the Crown and would produce colonial exports. Those who pretended to *sesmarias* were often squatters in the area, at least until the middle of the eighteenth century. They were always, however, individuals who possessed some form of wealth, most often Indian slaves, and social prestige. Invariably they were whites.

Below them were persons, ranked racially as whites, whose

connections to the grantees were close enough to obtain recognition of their squatter's rights within or along the boundaries of the *sesmarias*. These smallholders never dispensed with continued demonstrations of fealty to maintain their precarious rights. Without favor in the eyes of the grantees were those free persons who had more recently or more obviously, in terms of racial mixture, risen from among the population of "administered souls."

Over the course of the eighteenth century captive Indians gradually ceased to be treated as property. Their owners were enjoined by periodic laws, most notably that of 1758, to turn them over to public authorities for settlement in *aldeamentos*. Even though corrupt directors illegally leased them back to the same or other whites, the insecurity of control and continued racial mixing tended to turn the Indians into freedmen. The transformation of their status can be observed in censuses. At first listed as household property, they later were grouped in separate households, with last names corresponding to their tribal origin—"José Carijó," and the like. Their occupation often appears as *vive a favor*, "lives on favor," meaning by casual employment for others. One census taker entered under "Property": *bens nada sao gente vermelha, ou indios*, "no property they are red people, or Indians."[21]

Nevertheless new stocks of Indian slaves were intermittently added to the holdings of whites through raids for children or through purchases of children, if the tribe was desperate enough. As late as 1808 a royal order, contradicting earlier laws, encouraged the taking of Indian captives to hasten their acculturation, which, the order alleged, required "a hard school." The captor was granted ownership for fifteen years. Indians continued to be held under this order even after independence, and the practice was not legally abolished until 1831. Some Indians were still enslaved well after that date, however.[22] Meanwhile, the whites, as gold exports made them more affluent, could afford to replace their Indians with African slaves. Indeed, this development may be regarded as the principal reason for the gradual manumission of Indians; over the years some mulatto offspring of African slaves were also manumitted, or escaped, and mingled with the mestizo population.

Caipiras were available only for casual labor on the estates of the whites. They were reserved for certain tasks, especially the burning and preparation of new fields and mule driving. Intensive labor in the fields were performed by slaves, because the *caipiras* refused. In part, this division of labor was political, based on the whites need to surround themselves with persons who could be trusted to bear arms. It was also certainly the result of the frontier situation, which presented any free person with the alternative of squatting on unclaimed land. Estates could not offer wages effectively higher than subsistence yields because they were no more productive. The estates were inevitably less fertile than new swidden plots and presented only a slight degree of rationalization. Whites, however, preferred to regard the refusal of the *caipiras* to work steadily for them as definitive signs of laziness and improvidence.[23]

The leading edge of the frontier was therefore a *caipira* frontier, par excellence, composed of settlers practicing swidden and periodically subjected to eviction by persons of more political power and wealth. *Caipiras* were not disconnected from the economy of the white-controlled area. They planted for subsistence but preferred to settle along trade routes which permitted them to buy what they could not produce for themselves—mainly salt, which did not occur anywhere in the Paulista West, as well as knives, hoes, and firearms manufactured from iron deposits near Sorocaba and in Minas Gerais. Their stock in trade consisted of tobacco, salt pork, and live pigs, which were driven to the markets in the towns. They also supplied mule train drivers with rations of corn meal, manioc, and beans.

Those *caipiras* who preferred to confront the forest rather than remain on lands that had been appropriated made a "choice" which involved marginality of a terrifying completeness. Even though the social institutions of settled areas were controlled by the same persons who obtained land grants, nevertheless schools, churches, hospitals, and police performed essential functions. Liberation from the social hierarchy involved total abandonment. Travelers in *caipira* regions were repelled by what they presumed to call stupidity and apathy. They described a population ridden by parasitism and even subject to famine in years of crop failure.[24]

There is some evidence that the *caipira* frontier was useful to white social control. Judges often sentenced malefactors to banishment beyond the line of settlement. There they were joined by persons evading creditors, personal enemies, or the police. The frontier was also invaded by escaped African slaves, who sometimes formed communities, called *quilombos*. *Quilombos* were common in the interior of São Paulo, to judge from the frequency with which the word is encountered as a place name. The *caipiras* were generally hostile to the residents of the *quilombos*, and both were hostile to the tribal groups. The frontier was thus a place of far more violence than the settled areas. *Caipiras* sometimes fled from strangers, abandoning their dwellings and hiding in the forest at first approach.

It can be seen that the frontier of the *caipiras* was significantly integrated with the settlements of the plantations and towns.[25] It facilitated communication with the isolated mines of the far interior, provided the towns with certain trade goods, and served as a disposal area for persons who could not be integrated into the social order. The *caipiras* also formed a buffer zone against Indian attack, permitting the plantation owners and the state to economize military expenses.

Caipiras also added to the value of the land. It may be estimated that the clearing of a given acreage of primary forest doubled its price. Constant expropriation of squatter holdings thus obeyed an economic rationality. Only where the potential value of the land for export crops was slight, and where the *caipiras* were densely settled, were their prior rights recognized and their settlements allowed to survive and become the rural *bairros*, or neighborhoods, of the present day.

Until the coming of the railroad, São Paulo remained extremely rural. Most of the population clusters, and even many of the officially designated *vilas* (townships), were no larger in size than the Tupi-Guarani villages of 600 or so inhabitants. The city of São Paulo contained perhaps 6,000 persons who were not principally farmers, and the dozen or so larger townships reached their ceiling at 1,000 to 3,000. By the 1760s the attraction of the gold mines was beginning to lessen. The emigration which had held population nearly stable came to an end. In 1798 São Paulo's population reached 160,000, or about three per square kilometer, in the settled area, and the number of places designated as *vilas* rose to thirty-five.[26]

The Plantation Frontier

In the 1790s with the creation of sugar plantations, land exploitation significantly intensified. The Portuguese Crown, severely embarrassed by the decline of gold revenue and pressed by military necessity, began to encourage agricultural exports. The highlands of São Paulo were a difficult region to incorporate into overseas trade because the coastal escarpment exaggerated transport costs. Nevertheless, improved roads made possible an increasing flow of sugar exports after 1800.

Sugar was planted preferably in land cleared of primary forest. Towns at the edge of settlement therefore began to experience rapid growth. Itu and Porto Feliz, which still had some primary forest and were well connected by road to São Paulo, were the first planted in sugarcane. Campinas, beyond Jundiaí, and Piracicaba, beyond Itu, grew rapidly after 1800. By 1819 there were more than a hundred mills in Campinas. Most of the successful petitioners for *sesmarias* up to 1820 alleged that they were the owners of many slaves and intended to construct a mill. The cane-raising area by then had spread to Atibaia, Bragança, Mogi-Mirim, Limeira, and Capivári, all in an arc about 150 kilometers north of São Paulo.[27]

Sugarcane was planted from shoots and allowed to grow back after harvest for a second year. Replanting was then carried out and repeated for as many as ten years, after which the field was abandoned to allow native vegetation to take over. If the second growth (*capoeira*) was vigorous, sugar would be planted again after three years and the cycle followed until the cane finally failed. This was a much more intensive use of the soil than that practiced by swidden cultivators and caused a more rapid decline in humus content.

The amount of cultivated land per worker in sugarcane was much larger than that of subsistence farmers. Swidden clearings of eight-tenths hectare per person, which included about two-tenths hectare for trade goods, required about six hundred hours of labor per year.[28] The slaves therefore could provide for their own subsistence, barely, by work on their one "free" day each week—although some of their subsistence may have been produced during their regular work week. Since sugar cultivation was about as labor intensive as subsistence, slaves were available to work five or six times more land than subsistence farmers, for a total labor expenditure of an agonizing three thousand to thirty-five hundred hours per year. Since some slaves were diverted to the operation of the mill and transport, the sugar plantation probably burned about four times as much forest per capita as did swidden cultivation.

The mills themselves made heavy demands on the forest. Boiling down the syrup to a crystalline state consumed huge amounts of firewood. The extent of standing forest was therefore a major constraint on the continuation of sugar planting in a given region. In Itu a crisis was reached by 1830. Further advance into the forest was not practical because of transport costs. The mills required large numbers of oxen to power the grinding rollers and to bring the cane from the fields. In forested areas those beasts were underfed for lack of pasture. They were therefore worked to death rapidly and replaced as often as necessary.

Cultivation of sugar for export encouraged regional specialization, similar to that of the mines but on a smaller scale. Cattle ranches were formed around Franca and in the *campos* west of Botucatu, north of the basalt outcroppings. Other areas of highland *campo* nearer the sugar zone, near Avanhandava and Araraquara, were occupied only later, since cattle raised there would have had to be driven through forest. Most of the ranchers were emigrants from cattle-raising areas in Minas Gerais. Franca was 60 percent *mineiro* by 1824, and in the region of Campos Novos most of the land titles were taken by *mineiros*. Ranchers, like the planters, were evidently transferring considerable capitalized resources because they immediately assumed a social position superior to the *caipiras* and began to purchase slaves.[29]

Cattle ranching involved setting fire to the *campos*. The practice of burning became established as soon as the original cover had been grazed and trampled by cattle. Burning has the same effect in grassland as in forest: the mineral content of the vegetation enters the upper horizon of the soil, providing a sudden stimulus to new shoots, which the cattle prefer. Burning, however, must be followed immediately by rain to dissolve the minerals and transport them to the soil. Without rain the ashen material is lost to wind erosion. Even under the most favorable meteorological conditions, however, burning degrades the vegetation by interrupting succession and seasonal stages and favoring only those species which survive burning. It also impoverishes fauna, destroying nests, burrows, and young. The clayey soils, deprived of cover, were converted to laterite, a bricklike hardpan. The disappearance of anteaters and armadillos causes leaf-cutting ants to swarm. The leaf cutters, called *saúva* (*Atta* spp.) "eat more grass than the cows," as one observer lamented.[30]

Burning was employed not only at the beginning of the rainy season. It might be carried out whenever the owner wanted an immediate increase in forage, adding to the potential for rapid erosion. Already in 1819, the naturalist Saint-Hilaire, passing through Franca, mentioned a dust storm preceding a downpour of rain.[31] Burning of fields is an atavistic practice, yet it is easy to understand the alacrity with which fields are burned, once one has seen the marvelous carpet of new green shoots that spring up when burning is done just before the rains.

After independence the establishment of land titles changed drastically. The newly founded empire abolished *sesmarias* but found itself too weak to establish an alternate form of alienating public lands. This anomalous situation went on until 1850, when a law was passed declaring that henceforth public lands would be sold so that legal title would derive only from bills of sale emitted by the government. In the meantime, the frontier had advanced in the Paulista West by perhaps a hundred kilometers. Large expanses had been occupied without formalities. The law specified that these holdings would be recognized upon registration, if they were uncontested. Registration was carried out in São Paulo between 1855 and 1857.[32]

The legalization of squatter's rights, or *posses*, vastly accelerated private appropriations. The *sesmarias* had been astonishingly large—a square league "for the sustenance of my numerous and needy family" might become two or three leagues in the cattle regions. But there was no limit to what a locally powerful planter or rancher might claim in *posse*. One traveler in the 1850s found squatters at the confluence of the Grande and Paranaíba rivers who showed him "vast extents of backlands" and told him, "all that is my plantation." The legendary Mineiro José Teodoro de Souza laid claim to some twenty-five hundred square kilometers in the area of Campos Novos and was never challenged by police or courts.[33]

The law of 1850 had made some allowance for smallholding, particularly to encourage immigration, and was clearly opposed in principle to the further extension of the latifundia. Yet it was mocked by persons of wealth and power, who continued to engross public lands without payment or title. The eviction of *caipira* settlers, which this usurpation required, and the disputes among squatters generated "murders, looting, and devastation,"[34] which crested along the frontier. "Of all our laws," reported a government official, referring to *caipiras* located near Avanhandava in 1858, "they have a vague idea only about the one on lands, and that one they speak of with hostility and fear."[35]

The award of title to the most powerful and wealthy of the pretenders was the only function which the courts retained in this theft of public patrimony. Acquisition of title was, nevertheless, an essential final step in usurpation, since it added to the value of the land. Land was often sold without title—in fact such a sale might be a step in establishing a claim, since the buyers were thus bound to defend the pretentions of the original squatter. A title, however, reduced the risk of future legal claims. By a law in 1900, the state of São Paulo, which acquired federal lands by the Constitution of 1891, legalized all squatters' rights claimed after 1857. By then perhaps thirty thousand square kilometers of unclaimed public land remained; these, too, were usurped and the claims legalized by later state laws.[36]

No rights of the native Americans to tribal lands were ever recognized by the government of São Paulo. The law held that all of Brazil belonged to the state by right of conquest, to dispose of it as it wished. The *aldeamentos*, with their insufficient endowments of land, were a sort of grace which reverted to individually owned plots once the tribal group thus settled had become sufficiently acculturated. In fact, however, the lands of the *aldeamentos* were also encroached upon by whites.

A frontier may be considered the boundary between indigenous and invading peoples, a boundary which is pushed forward because the invaders possess techniques for the exploitation of nature which are more intensive and which therefore support a denser population. European expansionism, moreover, was impelled by the search for exports to send back to the metropolis to provide a profit to those who organized the colonizing effort. The frontier was therefore always an extractive frontier, not simply a frontier of settlement. The invasion of the Europeans was besides this an appropriation of land and natural resources which became part of a capital stock, owned by a relatively few people, who were thus enabled to dominate the frontier society.[37]

Sugarcane stimulated demographic expansion in São Paulo. By 1822 the census counted 345,000 persons—more than twice the number of a quarter-century earlier. Plantations had been founded as far west as Rio Claro, Araras, and Mogi-Mirim. In the Paraíba do Sul Valley, between São Paulo and Rio de Janeiro, a new crop, coffee, was growing in importance. By the 1830s it was the principal export of that region. Coffee was then brought to the Paulista West, hesitantly at first because of the fear of freezes. But the higher price of coffee converted the cane fields into coffee groves. Coffee was more valuable by weight and therefore cheaper to ship. It was also less subject to spoilage en route. Coffee was a transfer to Brazil some two centuries more recent than sugar. It had not encountered local parasites, nor had its Old-World parasites caught up with it. It was a member of the Rubiaceae and therefore relatively resistant to aluminum toxicity.

The coffee tree takes five years to come to maturity. Thereafter the trees produce for fifteen to forty years, depending on soil conditions. Growers tried to plant the coffee seedlings in the most appropriate soils; to this end they sought *padrões*, specimens of native tree species which required the same soil nutrients and absence of frost as coffee trees. Until the coffee trees reached maturity, subsistence crops were grown among them. Techniques of cultivation did not differ radically from swidden, in that the humus layer of the forest provided the necessary fertility. There was no fertilization, except that leaves and branches fallen to the ground were generally piled up around the trees to serve as mulch. The ground was hoed frequently to keep down weeds which competed for moisture. No other effort was made to maintain the mechanics or fertility of the soil and, given the nature of the slave regime, even these simple tasks were poorly executed.

Coffee production intensified in the Paulista West during the 1850s and 1860s, mainly in the areas in which cane had been raised. In the late 1860s and early 1870s there was a brief but profitable boom in cotton, caused by the elimination of the U.S. South from the world market. Population in the settled areas of São Paulo rose to 564,000 by 1854 and 837,000 by 1872, a density of 5–6 per square kilometers, nearly all of it still rural.[38]

By 1868 railroad construction was well advanced, and the final phase of occupation of the Paulista West had begun. A system of inclined planes and cable traction overcame the barrier of the coastal escarpment. The port of Santos was linked to the town of Jundiaí, about sixty kilometers beyond São Paulo. By the 1880s Itu, Sorocaba, Mogi-Mirim, and Araraquara were all connected with Santos via the city of São Paulo. The railroads continued to push forward into primeval forest. They followed the ridges between the parallel river basins, since the highlands not only were easier to traverse but also were the region of most fertile soil.[39] Rails dramatically opened the way for a huge increase in coffee production, until then restrained by the range of mule pack transport.

Paradoxically, a technologically advanced instrument made possible the extension of the most primitive agricultural techniques. Without the railroad, agriculture would have had to intensify in place. The locomotives were wood-burning, so they also represented a new demand upon primeval forest. The railroad facilitated the installation of stationary steam engines, also wood-burning, for textile spinning and weaving, coffee and grain milling, and most important, lumbering. The sawmills supplied railroad crossties and building materials.

From the early 1870s to 1900 the expansion of the coffee frontier was extremely rapid. The decadence of plantations in the Paraíba do Sul Valley, because of rapid erosion of their steep terrain, and the destruction of Asian coffee plantations by blight provoked a rapid increase in the value of potential coffee acreage in the Paulista West. The employment of African slaves had become more and more expensive after 1850, when the English had imposed an end

to the slave traffic. Rising slave prices in the coffee areas encouraged an interprovincial traffic, which, however, was insufficient to
the needs of the planters. Slaves in Brazil did not reproduce themselves, and those who were Brazilian-born were increasingly difficult to control. The crisis was finally resolved by abolition in 1888.
That act made São Paulo suddenly attractive to European emigrants, mainly Italians. Planters got the state to subsidize this flow
of workers. The 1890s therefore witnessed a huge inflow of population which continued, with fluctuations, to the mid-1920s and
pushed the frontier across the state line into Paraná.

The rapid advance of the frontier after the introduction of railroads and massive immigration was the result more of speculative
than of productive interests. The effective demand for coffee could
have been attended by a much more modest advance of the frontier, taking into consideration all the associated requirements for
subsistence crops and forage. By 1900 no more than fifteen thousand square kilometers was really needed for coffee plantations,
and even that area was exaggeratedly large because of overplanting.

Farming technique was little improved by the introduction of
wage labor. The self-interest of the workers lay in finding employment on plantations most recently opened. There they were allowed to plant between coffee rows, and there the soil was most
fertile. They would extract as much as possible from the land and
move on to another plantation. The plantation owner regarded his
land in similar fashion. Thus, the frontier was pushed forward fran-
tically and heedlessly.

Assault upon the Indians

The areas beyond *caipira* settlement had been largely though not
entirely cleared of tribal people by the early eighteenth century.
The expansion of whites into the *campos* of Mato Grosso and into
the Campos Gerais of Paraná required further attacks upon Indians, who retreated to the forests of Paraná and Paraguay and back
across the Paraná and Paranapanema rivers to the Paulista West.
Tribal groups residing in the region in the nineteenth century,
therefore, were peoples several times uprooted.

They depended considerably less on agriculture for subsis-

tence than had their ancestors. It is possible that they were revert-
ing to hunting and gathering because of an increased abundance of
game resulting from the disappearance of human predators during
the eighteenth century. It is also possible that the tribal groups had
made an adaptation to being themselves hunted by whites: they
were avoiding dependence on cultivated fields, which were so easily destroyed.[40] The returned tribal groups situated themselves
preferably along watercourses. This may have been a response to
the presence of *caipiras*, who avoided river bottoms out of fear of
the *sezões* (malaria or possibly typhoid). The Indians may also have
found an enlarged subsistence opportunity there. The increased
turbidity of the waters may have resulted in increased aquatic life.

The population of tribal peoples in mid-nineteenth-century São
Paulo was scattered and thin. To the north of the Tietê River were
Caiapó, and to the south were Kaingang and Oti-Xavante. In the
whole of the Paulista West therefore may have been only ten thousand tribal people occupying one hundred thousand square kilometers. Incursions of the whites caused some of these groups to sue
the government for peace. For these the policy of *aldeamentos* was
continued. A law of 1845 reformed these settlements and placed
them under the direction of Capuchin priests. By then, however,
the *aldeamentos* were already an anachronism, since the whites no
longer regarded the Indians brought to them as a useful labor pool.[41]

A flow of ranchers into the *campos* west of Botucatu created a
new situation of conflict. As long as the *caipiras* had borne the brunt
of Indian contact, the frontier had known periods of stability, during
which trade and cultural exchanges had taken place. By contrast,
the ranchers, whose cattle were extremely vulnerable to Indian attack, could not tolerate the presence of tribal people. Beginning
about 1860, they organized vigilante bands whose purpose was no
longer, as it had been fifty years before, to capture the Indians for
slaves. Now they sought simply to exterminate them. These bands,
casually formed from time to time, were called *dadas* or *batidas*.
The Indians had become *bugres*, a pejorative intense enough to
suggest a denial of their humanity, a transformation into varmints.
By the 1880s there had evolved the professional Indian killer, the
bugreiro. The tactic of the *batida* was to ambush villages at dawn.
Everyone, including women and children, was shot, and the huts

and fields were burned. Sometimes the huts were left intact, but the food stores were poisoned. Occasionally capitves were taken, especially women, who served the *bugreiros* as sexual slaves. The last male of the Oti-Xavante tribe was, in 1903, a slave. He had been captured and sold ten years before.[42]

Epilogue

The conquest of the first hundred thousand square kilometers of the Paulista West had taken three hundred years. The last hundred thousand took only fifty years. Large stands of forest were left in place and were only gradually cleared away. As late as 1920 about half of the area was still forested, but the introduction of heavy sawmills and trucks greatly intensified the exploitation of timber. The scattered stands of pine were quickly removed. *Caipira* subsistence farmers squatting in the forest continued to send valuable timber up in smoke, since they were without rights to use it or means to transport it. In some areas forest was burned to provide pasture, a procedure which seems the extremity of improvidence and waste but which is still being carried out in the Amazon Basin.[43]

Plantations were commonly converted into pasture once the yield of the coffee trees fell. The humus layer had been mined. One survey showed a loss of 75 percent in twenty-two years and an increase in acidity from pH 7.0 to 5.4.[44] Estates were sold off, fairly often in bankruptcy proceedings, for whatever they could fetch, to ranchers, who continued the process of degradation by removing the coffee groves and burning for pasture. The replacement of plantations with ranches produced the phenomenon of the "hollow frontier"—that is, of a population thinner behind the frontier than at its edge.

With the disappearance of habitats, hundreds of species of fauna also disappeared or became very rare in the region—monkeys, alligators, wildcats, parrots, toucans, deer, tapirs. The loss of this diversity was foreseen a century ago. One Paulista encountered, on a journey through forest, flocks of parrots "soaring and wheeling rudely and disagreeably overhead." The birds, he noted, were forest dwellers, and as the human population increased, "they will tend to emigrate, until one day they'll disappear." Indeed, the parrots were hunted commercially for the pet trade in Rio de Janeiro.[45]

Disappearance of the forest evoked little sense of loss, however. The European immigrant laborers had easily been contained on the plantations by their fear of the primeval forest. When they fled, it was to the city. White landowners had set the *caipiras* loose in the forest, to *desbravar*, "un-wild" it, and to *derrubar*, "defeat" it. Civilization was the cultural ideal, essentially urban, and even the tamed regularity of the farm fell short. For the Jesuits the forest had not displayed the presence of the deity—indeed it might be the abode of the devil—and as long as the indigenes had remained in it, refusing catechism, they were in his power.[46]

European travelers in São Paulo exhibited little curiosity concerning the forest. It is clear that they found their passage through it oppressive and fearsome, and they much preferred the *campos* and *cerrado*. No doubt their alienation arose partly from the strangeness of the flora. The colonists transformed the towns, not only with European fruit trees but also with European flowers and decorative plants, the better to restore their sense of place. The *caipiras* possessed at least a sense of belonging, the heritage of their Indian forebears. Their inseparability from nature is belied, perhaps, by their use of fire, but there is a mysterious power in the act of a mestizo backwoodsman observed by a French traveler. Spying along the river a deer he wished to kill, the part-Indian stripped off his clothes, the symbol of alienation from his prey, before he picked up his weapon.[47]

The fate of the São Paulo frontier was to be despoiled of its easily exploitable resources and to suffer extreme degradation of its ecosystems. The process was nevertheless regarded by those who accomplished it as a brilliant achievement. It was accompanied by genocide. It did not result in a broadening of human potentialities of the victors, since it replicated, and even caricatured, the inequality of the metropolis. It is true that the export of coffee made possible the importation of an array of human and capital resources that soon produced a higher level of material standards, but this form of development thereafter suffered the consequences of a weakened agricultural base. In the wake of severe environmental degradation, the successors of the original settlers have undertaken to manage their remaining resources rationally. Nevertheless, extractive practices and attitudes have persisted into the present because the frontier itself continued its march into Paraná, Mato Grosso, Goiás and beyond, to the borders of Peru and Colombia.

NOTES

1. Assistance for research in connection with this article was provided by the American Philosophical Society.

2. Fundacão Instituto Brasileiro de Geografia e Estatística, *Geografia do Brasil*, vol. III, *Região Sudeste* (Rio de Janeiro: FIBGE, 1977), pp. 51–86; José Setzer, *Atlas climatológico e ecologico do estado de São Paulo* (São Paulo: Comissão Interestadual da Bacia Paraná-Uruguay, 1966).

3. FIGBE, *Geografia do Brasil*, III, 10–46.

4. Ibid., III, 91–116.

5. Pierre Monbeig, *Pionniers et planteurs* (Paris: A. Colin, 1952), pp. 71–75.

6. Robert Goodland and Mario Ferri, *Ecologia do cerrado* (Belo Horizonte: Livraria Itatiaia, 1979), pp. 13–59; Monbeig, *Pionniers et planteurs*, p. 75; Setzer, *Atlas climatológico*, p. 51; Carlos Toledo Rizzini, *Tratado de fitogeografia do Brasil* (São Paulo: HUCITEC, 1976), pp. 13–155.

7. An attempted solution to the problem, based on toponymy, is Helmut Troppmair, *A cobertura vegetal primitivo do estado de São Paulo* (São Paulo: Instituto de Geografia, 1969). The method does not take into account changes which occurred before the name was bestowed. The map accompanying the study is too small to judge the result; however, the method is interesting. It may be noted that land grants, *sesmarias*, provide information on vegetation in some cases. Compilation of this information would be a laborious but worthwhile process. See Arquivo Público do Estado de São Paulo, Sesmarias, Patentes e Provisões.

8. Quoted in Rizzini, *Tratado de fitogeografia*, p. 88; Ezechias Paulo Heringer mentions sixteen hundred years; "Propagacão e sucessão de espécies arbóreas do cerrado em funcão do fogo, do cupim, da capina, e do Aldrin," in *III simpósio sobre o cerrado*, ed. M. G. Ferri (São Paulo: Edgard Blücher, 1971), p. 167.

9. On fauna, see C. de Mello Leitão, *Zoogeografia do Brasil* (São Paulo: Cia. Editora Nacional, 1947).

10. Egon Schaden, *Aspectos fundamentais da cultura Guarani* (São Paulo: DIFEL, 1962).

11. Auguste de Saint-Hilaire, *Viagem à província de São Paulo* (Belo Horizonte: Livraria Itatiaia, 1976), pp. 56, 120.

12. Pasquale Petrone, "Os aldeamentos paulistas e sua funcão na valorizacão da região paulistana," *livre-docência* thesis, Department of Geography, University of São Paulo, 1964, ch. 1.

13. Luiz Felipe Baeta Neves, *O combate dos soldados de Cristo na terra dos papagaios* (Rio de Janeiro: Forense, 1979), pp. 130–32.

14. Egon Schaden, *Aculturacão indígena* (São Paulo: Livraria Pioneira, 1969), pp. 179–88.

15. Sergio Buarque de Holanda, *Expansão paulista em fins do século XVI e princípio do século XVII* (São Paulo: Instituto de Administracao, 1948); Luci de

Abreu Maffei and Arlinda Rocha Nogueira, "O ouro na capitania de S. Vincente nos séculos XVI e XVII," *Anais do Museu Paulista*, 20 (1966): 7–136.

16. Afonso d'Escragnolle Taunay, *História das bandeiras paulistas*, 3d ed. (São Paulo: Melhoramentos, 1975); Richard Morse, *The Bandeirantes* (New York: Alfred A. Knoff, 1966).

17. Afonso d'Escragnolle Taunay, *Relatos sertanistas* (São Paulo: Livraria Martins, 1953), p. 181; Aluisio de Almeida, "Achegas à história do sul paulista," *Revista do Arquivo Municipal*, 6, no. 69 (1940): 157–58.

18. Sergio Buarque de Holanda, *Monções*, 2d ed. (São Paulo: Alfa Ômega, 1976).

19. J. B. von Spix and C. F. P. von Martius, *Viagem pela capitania de S. Paulo* (São Paulo: Diario Oficial, 1929), p. 56.

20. Altiva Pilatti Balhanna, et al., *Campos Gerais: Estruturas agrárias* (Curitiba: Faculdade de Filosofía, 1968), p. 30.

21. Excursão . . . Gal. Rodrigo de Menezes, 1737, Instrucão, Tempos Coloniais, 88, Arquivo Público do Estado de São Paulo; População Mogi-Mirim, Tempos Coloniais, 116, ibid.; Mario Neme, *Apossamento do solo e evolução da propriedade rural na zona de Piracicaba* (São Paulo: Museu Paulista, 1974), pp. 62–65.

22. Notices on Indian slaves, 1826, Ofícios Diversos, Campinas, Tempos Imperiais, 849, Arquivo Público do Estado de São Paulo; João Francisco Tidei Lima, "A ocupação da terra e a destruição dos índios na região de Bauru," master's thesis, Department of History, Universidade de São Paulo, 1978, pp. 75–79.

23. Antonio Rodrigues Velloso de Oliveira, *Memoria sobre o melhoramento da Provincia de S. Paulo* (Rio de Janeiro: Typographia Nacional, 1822), p. 29.

24. Luiz d'Alincourt, *Memoria sobre a viagem do porto de Santos à cidade de Cuiabá* (Belo Horizonte: Livraria Itatiaia, 1975), p. 59; Saint-Hilaire, *Viagem à São Paulo*, p. 85.

25. On *caipira* marginality, see Octavio Guilherme Velho, *Capitalismo autoritário e campesinato* (São Paulo: DIFEL, 1976), pp. 116–17.

26. Maria Luiza Marcílio, *A cidade de São Paulo* (São Paulo: Pioneira, 1974), p. 25.

27. José Jobson de Andrade Arruda, "O Brasil no comêrcio colonial (1796–1808)," Ph.D. diss., Department of History, Universidade de São Paulo, 1972, pp. 229–31; Maria Thereza Schorer Petrone, *A lavoura canavieira em São Paulo* (São Paulo: DIFEL, 1968), pp. 9–23.

28. See estimates in Warren Dean, *Rio Claro: A Brazilian Plantation System* (Stanford: Stanford University Press, 1976), p. 9.

29. von Spix and von Martius, *Viagem pela capitania*, pp. 66, 85; População Franca, Tempos Coloniais, 44, Arquivo Público do Estado de São Paulo.

30. José Arouche de Toledo Rondon, *Obras* (São Paulo: Perspectiva, 1978), p. 7.

31. Saint-Hilaire, *Viagem à São Paulo*, p. 86.

32. Warren Dean, "Latifundia and Land Policy in Imperial Brazil," *Hispanic American Historical Review*, 51, no. 4 (Nov., 1971).

33. Amador Nogueira Cobra, *Em um recanto do sertão paulista* (São Paulo: Hennies, 1923).

34. Antonio Mariano de Azevedo, *Relatorio . . . sobre os exames de que foi incumbido no interior da provincia de S. Paulo* (Rio de Janeiro: Typographia Nacional, 1858), p. 45.

35. Ibid.

36. Monbeig, *Pionniers et planteurs*, pp. 125–26; São Paulo (State), *Terras devolutas e particulares no Estado de São Paulo* (São Paulo: Diario Oficial, 1912); João Pedro da Veiga Filho, *Estudo economico e financeiro sobre o estado de S. Paulo* (São Paulo: Diario Official, 1896), p. 30.

37. Leo Waibel, "As zonas pioneiras do Brasil," *Revista Brasileira de Geografia*, 17, no. 4 (1955): 400; José de Souza Martins, "Frente pioneira: Contribuicão para uma caracterizacão sociológica," *Estudos Históricos*, 10 (1971): 30; Gervasio Castro de Rezende, "Plantation Systems, Land Tenure and Labor Supply: An Historical Analysis of the Brazilian Case with a Contemporary Study of the Cacao Region of Bahia, Brazil," Ph.D. diss., Department of Economics, University of Wisconsin, Madison, 1976.

38. On the coffee frontier, see Sergio Milliet, *Roteiro de café e outros ensaios* (São Paulo: Departamento de Cultura, 1939); and Ary Franca, *A marcha do cafe e as frentas pioneiras* (Rio de Janeiro: Conselho Nacional de Geografia, 1960).

39. Amadeu de Queiroz, "São Paulo e o sul de Minas," *Revista do Arquivo Municipal*, 3, no. 40 (1937): 187–200.

40. Teodoro Sampaio, *São Paulo no século XIX e outros ciclos históricos* (Petrópolis: Vozes, 1978), pp. 110–22.

41. Baron of Antonina to President of Province, 1872, TI, Policia, No. 110, Arquivo Público do Estado de São Paulo; Tidei Lima, "A ocupacão daterra," p. 87.

42. Tidei Lima, "A ocupacão da terra," pp. 136–42.

43. "A devastação florestal," *Estado de São Paulo*, January 21, 1979; "A agricultura em S. Paulo," *Boletim do Departamento Estadual de Estatística*, nos. 3–4 (1920): 55.

44. Monbeig, *Pionniers et planteurs*, pp. 78–79.

45. Salvador José Correa Coelho, *Passeio à minha terra* (São Paulo: Typographia da Lei, 1860), p. 76.

46. Baeta Neves, *O combate*, pp. 51, 63.

47. Antonio Cândido, *Os parceiros do Rio Bonito* (Rio de Janeiro: José Olympio, 1964), p. 64, quoting Hercules Florence.

The Southern African Frontier in Comparative Perspective

THE dominant tradition in American frontier historiography ema-
nates from the work of Frederick Jackson Turner, whose ideas were
formulated in an ethos dominated by late-nineteenth-century social
Darwinism, American nationalism, and Midwest regionalism. Turner's formulation contains numerous insights of permanent value,
but his work has serious flaws. First, he contended that the American frontier experience was unique and that it is therefore incom-
parable. Though everything is in some sense unique, every thing is
also related to other things in systematic and comparable ways.
Second, Turner saw the history of the American frontier exclusively
from the point of view of the white intruders. However, the indigenous Indian peoples were also key actors in the frontier process.
Third, Turner described American frontier society as egalitarian. As
George Orwell would have said, even among whites, some were
distinctly more equal than others.[1] These flaws continue to crop up
in the works of Turner's latter-day disciples, including Ray Allen
Billington.[2]

   At the other extreme, there are historians who apply the term
frontier to such heterogeneous circumstances, without definition
or taxonomic order, that they deprive it of intellectual rigor. If one
judges by its newsletters and by the book published under its aus-
pices in 1977, that is the weakness of the Oklahoma school of frontier history. *The Frontier: Comparative Studies* is a series of scholarly and often interesting essays on situations as disparate as the
Roman Empire and modern Brazil, but each author was allowed to
attach his own meaning to the term *frontier*, and the relationships
between the essays are not apparent.[3]

   Since 1971, Professor Howard Lamar and I have been grap-
pling with these problems in a series of graduate seminars at Yale

University, with the cooperation of a succession of talented graduate students and visiting scholars. In 1981 we published *The Frontier in History: North America and Southern Africa Compared*,[4] with contributions from American and southern African specialists. The rest of this essay owes much to that joint work.

While we consider that Walter Prescott Webb stretched the frontier concept beyond its appropriate limits, we admire him for having counteracted the principal flaws in the Turner tradition.[5] The basic problem is to define and describe a concept that is not culture-bound and that nevertheless has content specific enough to be a useful tool for analyzing and illuminating significant historical processes. In our usage, a frontier is an area of interpenetration between societies. It contains three elements: a territorial element, a zone or territory as distinct from a boundary line; a human element, comprising peoples of initially separate and distinct societies; and the process by which relations among such peoples commence, develop, and eventually crystallize. A frontier opens with the first contact between the members of two societies. It closes when a single authority has established political and economic hegemony over the zone. When we talk of a frontier closing, we do not imply that the relations between the inhabitants then become static or rigid, but rather that a new structural situation has been created and the ongoing historical process is no longer a frontier process.

If the frontier concept is to have general applicability, and not to be culture-bound, one should not assume that an intrusive society necessarily emerges as the winner in the struggle for power in a frontier zone. Even in the period of European expansion there were many cases in which white intruders were palpably the losers, as with the Raleigh settlement in Virginia. Moreover, distinguishing winners from losers is not always a simple matter but depends upon one's time frame. At a given moment one segment of a society may be winning and another losing, but the winners of that generation may be the losers in the next.

There are many types of frontiers. Interacting societies may have similar or different technological levels and modes of production. The amount of technological differentiation between societies is one key variable in a frontier situation. It often, but not invariably, determines the outcome of a struggle for power in a frontier zone. The occupations of participants in a frontier zone form a second key variable. There is, for example, a great difference between a zone in which the intrusive element consists of transients who continue to regard their country of origin as their home and one which includes settlers who intend to found permanent homes in the frontier zone for themselves and their descendants. The ultimate decision-makers in a metropole may have a weak or a strong commitment to a frontier zone. The extent of commitment of each of the interacting societies is a third key variable. These variables may change over time. In an early phase a few peripatetic traders or a few missionaries with very little influence over their metropolitan governments may be the only representatives of an intrusive society in a frontier zone, but the stake of members in the metropolitan society may then increase to the stage at which its government becomes committed in an all-out effort to gain control of the territory.

We should also distinguish different levels of abstraction at which to examine frontier processes. At the highest level, one might take cognizance of everything that is discernible about every sort of frontier in the entire human experience; in that case we would recognize that all empires, most states, and many acephalous societies have generated frontier processes. At an intermediate level, one might confine the scope to great themes that have limits in time or in space or in typology. One might compare the histories of the frontiers of the great pre-Cartesian empires of Rome and China or the frontiers of nonliterate societies or frontiers created by specific occupational groups such as traders, missionaries, or settlers. Or again, one might follow Walter Prescott Webb and focus on the frontiers created by the expansion of Europeans and of commercial and industrial capitalism in the modern era, or on a regional example of such frontiers as North America or southern Africa. Finally, at the micro-level, small areas might be studied in depth over short periods to reveal the great complexities that exist whenever fragments of originally separate and distinct societies interact with each other, as in seventeenth-century New England or Virginia.[6]

My mandate for this paper is to discuss the frontier in southern African history. If I were to deal with all frontier processes that we know to have existed in the region, I should certainly include those

created by the expansion of pastoralists (Khoikhoi or "Hottentots")
into areas previously inhabited exclusively by hunter-gatherers (San
or "Bushmen") and also those created by the infiltration of Bantu-
speaking mixed farmers into the eastern part of southern Africa,
where they interacted with the pastoralists and hunter-gatherers.
However, after brief references to those processes that had occurred before da Gama's time, I propose to treat southern Africa as
a regional example of the frontiers created by the expansion of Europe and of the capitalist economy, which is a large enough theme.

The Southern African Environment and the Phases of White Expansion

Southern Africa is predominantly an arid region. Before the discovery of diamonds and gold, and the introduction of industrial technology in the second half of the nineteenth century, rainfall was the
most valued resource—and its incidence varies tremendously. Most
of the western three-fifths of the region has an average of less than
twenty inches of rain a year and was not suitable for arable farming
with preindustrial technology. The exception is the Cape peninsula,
its immediate hinterland, and the adjacent coastal strip to its east,
where grain could have been cultivated because there are reliable
winter rains. The eastern two-fifths of the region has an average of
more than twenty inches of rain a year, nearly all of it falling in
summer. Although there are considerable variations from year to
year and intermittent periods of prolonged drought, crop production is generally feasible except in the mountains, the most formidable of which form an escarpment within a hundred miles of the
Indian Ocean, rising to over eleven thousand feet above sea level
in the Drakensberg. Most of southern Africa is free of the human
and animal diseases that are the scourge of tropical Africa, but in
the coastal lowlands and the river valleys of the northern and eastern parts of the region, anopheles mosquitos undermined human
health and tsetse flies made pastoral farming impossible.[7]

The best natural harbors in southern Africa are in the Cape
peninsula; but Table Bay is exposed to the northwest winds that
prevail in winter, frequently reaching gale force, while False Bay is
exposed to the summer southeaster. None of the river mouths are

penetrable by ocean-going ships without extensive dredging, and all the rivers are obstructed by cascades as the land rises steeply towards the mountain escarpment.

These factors profoundly influenced the history of southern Africa both before and after the beginning of white colonization. By the time of Vasco da Gama, the western sector was sparsely occupied by people whose ancestors had probably lived in the region for many millennia. Some lived in small bands as hunter-gatherers; others possessed sheep and cattle, were organized in larger communities, and occupied the better pasturelands, especially those in the winter rainfall area. All these people formed a relatively closed, isolated population. Whites were to call the hunter-gatherers *Bushmen* and the pastoralists *Hottentots*, but those terms have acquired such derogatory connotations that it is preferable to use the indigenous terms *San* and *Khoikhoi*, or to refer to those people jointly as Khoisan.

Members of a different genetic population had infiltrated from the north into the eastern sector of the region since early in the Christian era. They constituted the southernmost prong of a continental movement that probably originated in eastern Nigeria. They spoke related Bantu languages, they made iron tools and weapons, they cultivated sorghum and vegetables as well as herding sheep and cattle, and they were organized in cohesive, autonomous chiefdoms, some of which included as many as fifty thousand people. By the time of da Gama, their iron-working, mixed-farming culture prevailed throughout most of the eastern part of southern Africa. Some of the Khoisan peoples had been driven into mountain refuges or westward into the arid territories beyond the twenty-inch rainfall line. Many had been incorporated into the farming communities, with the result that the Bantu-speaking peoples of southern Africa had acquired Khoisan genes and several Khoisan cultural traits, including the use of clicks in their languages.

Before Europeans began to sail round the Cape, a frontier zone between Bantu-speaking mixed farmers and Khoisan hunters and herders ran northward from the vicinity of the Fish River to the Molopo River and beyond, following approximately the twenty-inch rainfall line that set a limit to arable farming. In the coastal part of that zone, on either side of the Fish River, the Xhosa chiefdoms

were gradually overcoming and incorporating the easternmost
Khoikhoi, but they did not break through the arid area around
modern Port Elizabeth to occupy the rich winter rainfall lands of
the southwestern Cape.[8]

When the directors of the Dutch East India Company decided
to found a way station on the southern African mainland to service
their fleets on passage between Europe and Indonesia, they selected the Cape peninsula for its harbors and its climate. That decision initiated a frontier process between Europeans and the Khoisan
peoples. Its history falls into two phases, distinguished by environmental factors. In the first phase, from 1652 to about 1713, the
frontier zone extended about seventy-five miles northward and forty-
five miles eastward from Cape Town through much of the area of
good winter rains. White colonists occupied land at the expense of
Khoikhoi pastoralists and used it to produce wine and wheat as well
as sheep and cattle. The Khoikhoi of that area quite rapidly lost
their livestock and with them their capacity to preserve their autonomy. Often they bartered sheep or cattle with company officials or
colonists in exchange for copper, tobacco, or brandy; sometimes
Europeans seized livestock by force. On three occasions Khoikhoi
went to war, but they were quite easily overcome. The effects of
European firearms were compounded by internal divisions among
the Khoikhoi and their lack of strong leadership. The *coup de grace*
came in 1713, when a smallpox epidemic swept away many Khoikhoi. Thereafter the arable area near Cape Town lay inside the frontier and was firmly controlled by Europeans. The Khoikhoi survivors who remained there were working for Europeans as farm
laborers and domestic servants.[9]

By the turn of the century, colonists were beginning to open
up a very different type of frontier in the arid territories north and
east of the arable belt. Despite the fact that in 1700 there were still
fewer than twelve hundred European men, women, and children
in the colony, they were already producing more grain and wine
than could be absorbed by the market, which was limited to the
needs of passing ships and the inhabitants of the town. Moreover,
arable land was becoming expensive, capital was scarce, and slaves
were being imported from tropical Africa, Madagascar, and Southeast Asia to perform manual and artisan work in the town and on

Southern Africa in the Nineteenth Century

the farms. Except for a limited number of farmers, innkeepers and petty traders, there was no way of life within the arable area that the European colonists found acceptable; but there *was* an outlet in the territories beyond, where a man could set himself up as a *trekboer* (stockfarmer) with a little capital or, if he lacked even that, could become a *bijwoner* (tenant) of a *trekboer*. The government facilitated rapid expansion into those territories by permitting colonists to occupy large tracts of land for very low annual rents and even, in time, allowing them to treat such holdings as marketable properties.

During the eighteenth century the European population of the colony grew quite rapidly, by natural increase rather than fresh immigration, to reach about twenty thousand by the end of the century. The greater part became *trekboers*, who spread outwards with flocks of sheep toward the Orange River in the north and the Fish River in the east, each family occupying six thousand or more acres and tending to move on when they had exhausted the meager pastures.[10]

The Khoikhoi inhabitants, demoralized by the conquest of their fellow pastoralists in the southwestern Cape and by successive smallpox epidemics in 1713, 1755, and 1767, offered relatively little resistance. As they in turn lost their livestock and their control over water supplies, their chiefdoms broke up into small family groups, most of whom became clients of *trekboers*, herding their sheep and doing their domestic work. Aboriginal hunters tried to preserve their autonomy by raiding *trekboer* livestock from time to time, but they did not impede white expansion except in the northeastern frontier zone, where, from bases in the Sneeuwberg, they harassed the colonists sufficiently to check their advance until the second decade of the nineteenth century.[11]

The environment affected this phase of white expansion in three ways. It made it possible for a few thousand white people to consolidate a bridgehead in the Cape peninsula and to occupy a territory as large as Great Britain before they came up against the numerous and powerful Bantu-speaking mixed farmers. Second, the aridity of the area made it necessary for the whites who moved out from the arable southwest to become extensive stock farmers. And third, since the Cape peninsula contained the only good natural harbors, expanding white society formed a single economic, political, and cultural continuum, whereas in North America, as later in Australia, there were several points of entry from the sea and as many different social and economic networks and subcultures.

By 1770 the eastern fringe of the colonial society was impinging on the western fringe of the African mixed-farming society on either side of the twenty-inch rainfall line. This was the beginning of a long struggle for control of the fertile eastern two-fifths of southern Africa. For the next forty years the Zuurveld, to the west of the Fish River, was a typical frontier zone. White pastoralists and Xhosa mixed farmers were intermingling there and fighting a series of inconclusive wars. In 1812, however, deploying imperial troops as well as colonial levies, the British made a decisive advance, driving twenty thousand Xhosa across the Fish River and effectively closing the Zuurveld frontier zone. Thereafter the whites, with professional soldiery and superior firepower, advanced beyond the Fish. A typical war started with an African attack, intended to avenge previous defeats, and ended when white forces had swept deep into Xhosa territory, destroying crops and seizing cattle. In 1856, having sustained a series of such defeats in 1819, 1834–35, 1846–47, and 1850–53, many Xhosa resorted to a supernatural, millennial remedy. They killed their cattle and destroyed their grain in the belief that such a demonstration of confidence in the power of their ancestors would cause the disappearance of white people. In fact, the result was mass starvation and the subjection of the survivors to white control.[12]

Meanwhile, several thousand *trekboers* (later known as voortrekkers) had left the Cape Colony with the intention of carving out new homes for themselves and establishing governments independent of Great Britain in the eastern part of southern Africa.[13] At that time the *mfecane* wars, launched by the Zulu king, Shaka, and his Ndebele rival, Mzilikazi, had devastated and partially depopulated much of the fertile grassland on the high veld between the Maloti Mountains and the Limpopo River, as well as many square miles of the lowlands in Natal, south of the Tugela River.[14] The Ndebele and the Zulu attempted to prevent the voortrekkers from settling in those areas, but the voortrekkers warded off mass African onslaughts by lashing their wagons together to form defensive *laa-*

gers and then went over to the attack, driving the Ndebele north-
wards across the Limpopo River and defeating Dingane's Zulu regiments. After that the whites were able to found settlements in
Natal and on the high veld on both sides of the Vaal River.[15]

By 1870, Natal had become a British colony with a few thousand settlers from the British Isles, and the voortrekkers were expanding from several different nuclear settlements on the high veld
at the expense of their African neighbors in a series of frontier zones.
The most fiercely contested expansion was into the fertile Caledon
River Valley, where the Basotho under their founder, King Moshweshwe, resisted Afrikaner penetration for many years before losing control of the land on the northern side of the river and accepting white over-rule in 1868.[16] Even so, in 1870 large areas were
still controlled by autonomous African chiefdoms. The colony of
Natal had a revitalized Zulu kingdom to its north and Mpondo and
other chiefdoms to its south, and the voortrekker republic in the
Transvaal was almost surrounded by independent African communities—the Tswana to its west; the Swazi, the Pedi, the Tsonga,
and others to its east; and the Venda to its north, with a reconsti-
tuted Ndebele kingdom across the Limpopo River. For a while,
environmental factors as well as African power set limits to white
expansion. In particular, mosquitos and tsetse flies prevented Afrikaners from founding durable settlements in the low veld of the
eastern Transvaal and from creating a trade route through southern
Mozambique to the sea at Delagoa Bay and thus breaking the monopoly of their external trade by British colonial merchants and
their agents.

After 1870, whites rapidly established hegemony over the remaining African communities.[17] The British mounted a major expedition to conquer the Zulu in 1879 after losing an entire regiment
at Isandhlwana.[18] The Pedi and the Venda defied the Transvaal Boers
for many years before they were finally subdued in the last decade
of the century. On the other hand, the Mpondo, the Swazi, and
most of the Tswana chiefdoms submitted to white authorities without a fight after they had been nearly encircled by white-controlled
territories. Nevertheless, whites in the eastern part of southern Africa did not actually farm much land beyond what had been devastated during the *mfecane* wars in the 1820s. Africans maintained

effective occupation of most of the land in the Transkei, Lesotho (Basutoland), kwaZulu (Zululand), and Botswana (Bechuanaland Protectorate) and considerable blocks in the Ciskei, Natal, Swaziland, and the Transvaal.[19]

After 1885 another frontier was created in the heart of the Transvaal Boer republic, following the discovery of gold in the Witwatersrand. This was an entirely different type of frontier. Johannesburg became the core of an agressive urban society, where European capitalists dominated a labor force divided sharply between well-paid European artisans and low-paid African migrant laborers. The Africans shuttled between their rural homes and the mines, where they stayed for about a year at a time and were limited to unskilled tasks. This industrial society bore outwards upon the surrounding agrarian society, where Boer landowners dominated their African labor-tenants much as their ancestors had dominated Khoikhoi clients in the Cape Colony before the Great Trek.[20]

The Role of Metropolitan Governments

Before 1870, southern Africa was of secondary importance in the Dutch and British imperial systems. Dutch and British businessmen valued the Cape peninsula for its strategic position between Europe and the sources of spices in Southeast Asia. Beyond what was necessary to maintain an efficient refreshment station in the peninsula, and to prevent rivals from capturing it, they had no major interest in southern Africa, because the region was not known to contain significant resources.

For over a century and a half, Dutch and British officials sought to give effect to this perspective by keeping their colonists within prescribed boundaries. In the 1650s, Jan van Riebeeck, the first commander, planted an almond hedge to confine the colony to a portion of the Cape peninsula. Officials also considered digging a canal across the Cape flats to separate the peninsula from the mainland. Later governors laid down a succession of boundary lines leading inland from points on the southeast coast. Finally, after defeating the Xhosa in 1812, the British built forts along the Fish River. Colonists were prohibited from crossing these successive official boundaries, but all such proclamations were dead letters, be-

cause the same economic considerations that caused the metropolitan governments to wish to limit the area of European settlement
also prevented them from creating a bureaucracy strong and independent enough to exact compliance from the colonists.

The Dutch East India Company kept nearly all its personnel
in the peninsula. Elsewhere, it did establish district offices at Stellenbosch in 1679, Swellendam in 1746, and Graaff-Reinet in 1786,
but it staffed each of them with only one general-purpose official
(*landdrost*), a clerk or two, and at most a handful of soldiers. The
landdrosts were instructed to administer their vast districts. In
practice beyond the Cape peninsula, however, and more particularly beyond the arable belt, the government possessed scarcely
any instruments for exerting its authority on a regular basis, though
as a last resort it could bring the colonists to heel by cutting off
their ammunition supplies. Consequently, the *trekboers* lived as
semiautonomous family units, bartering their farm produce and sheep
and cattle with traveling traders in exchange for firearms and ammunition and modest quantities of clothing, groceries, and brandy.
They devised their own system of defense, forming commandos under their own elected officers to deal with aboriginal hunting bands
who preyed on their herds, and they could usually ignore with impunity proclamations that were intended to limit their movements
or moderate their dealings with their slaves and their Khoisan clients.
There was also nothing to stop Bantu-speaking Africans from entering the colony, and by the end of the eighteenth century the pe-
ripheries of the colonial society and the African farming society were
intermingled in a board frontier zone on either side of the Fish
River—the beginning of a process that proved to be irreversible.[21]

The Batavian regime (1803–1806) and its British successor did
make some efforts to strengthen the local administration by dividing the colony into smaller districts and sending judges on circuit
to hear cases at the district headquarters. In the 1830s, however,
the British failed to prevent the voortrekkers from leaving the colony. They merely made halfhearted attempts to form alliances with
the brown and black rulers of the states through which the voortrekkers traveled—Griqua states and Moshweshwe's Lesotho—but
these devices did not hinder the voortrekkers from penetrating to
the central high veld. In the 1850s, after a disastrous short-lived

attempt to exercise authority over a vast area between the Orange and the Vaal rivers, the British withdrew. They repudiated their treaty commitments to the brown and black rulers and granted sweeping political powers to the whites in the form of representative parliamentary institutions in the Cape Colony and Natal and outright independence to the voortrekker communities, who formed independent republics on either side of the Vaal River.[22]

After 1870, British policy in southern Africa became decidedly expansionist, especially when the Conservative (or Unionist) party was in power. Colonization had already generated forces that favored imperial expansion in the region. The British immigrants who had settled in Natal and the eastern part of the Cape Colony looked to the metropolitan government to support their interests against those of Africans and Afrikaners. The traders who exchanged imported goods for wool, ivory, and other local products in the interior; the bankers and merchants in Cape Town, Port Elizabeth, East London, and Durban on whom the traders depended; and the London and other British houses with which they in turn were associated all tended to believe that imperial advances into areas occupied by Africans and Afrikaners would protect and enhance their interests. Missionaries, too, used their influence with the evangelical network in Britain to promote imperial expansion, assuming that a British regime would provide a climate conducive to evangelization and give Africans some protection from the rapacity of white laymen. Moreover, many, and probably most, of the imperial officials and senior military officers who served in southern Africa were expansionists.

Previously, pressures from such sources had been tempered by the resistance of the British taxpayer to unremunerative commitments. Now, however, with capital pouring into southern Africa for the development of the mining industries, with scientific racism pervasive in western culture, and with other European nations making claims to African territories, the expansionist forces gathered momentum, coming to a climax at the turn of the century.[23]

Great Britain played an active role in the subjection of the remaining African chiefdoms—notably in the Zulu war of 1879, which was a clearcut case of imperial aggression—and, after annexing the Transvaal in 1877 and disannexing it in the face of Afrikaner resistance four years later, Britain became involved in a major war to conquer the two republics in 1899. After 1905, however, Great Britain abandoned the effort to exert political control over the region, and with it surrendered the only levers she had possessed that might have safeguarded the interests of the black majority. A Liberal government gave responsible government to the white inhabitants of the former republics and encouraged their politicians to join with those of Natal and the Cape Colony to form a united, self-governing British dominion, which was inaugurated in 1910. The frontier era in southern African ended thus, with a concentration of political power in the hands of the local white population, who shared economic power with metropolitan capitalists.[24]

Institutions

The eighteenth century was the period when European colonists in southern Africa became Afrikaners as they adapted to an environment that differed profoundly from northwestern Europe. The most distinctive changes took place in the rapidly expanding frontier zones, where *trekboers* acquired traits that would persist among their descendants in the nineteenth century and leave traces still discernible today.

The typical *trekboer* social unit was a patriarchal family of two or three generations, served by several Khoikhoi client families and perhaps a slave or two, occupying more than six thousand acres of land and owning several hundred sheep and a few head of cattle. The nearest shop and government office might be several hundred miles away at Stellenbosch, after 1745 at Swellendam, or, by the end of the century, at Graaff Reinet, across country that could only be traversed on foot, on horseback, or laboriously over rough tracks by ox-wagon. Since Cape Town remained the only port of entry into the colony, a *trekboer* became more divorced from European culture, Dutch political authority, and the market economy the farther he trekked from Cape Town.[25]

The government appointed several men (*heemraden*) to assist a *landdrost*—for example, to sit with him in a district court to adjudicate petty civil disputes. The government also appointed *veldkornets* as its agents in each subdivision of a district. But criminal cases could only be tried in Cape Town and *heemraden* and *veldkornets* were part-time, unpaid officials—influential members of the *trekboer* community, whose interests they represented and prejudices they shared.[26] For defense—and often for aggression—against the aborigines whose hunting and collecting grounds they were occupying, the able-bodied men of a locality joined together to form commandos, and the government supplied them with ammunition and recognized the officers they elected.[27] Consequently, if the Cape officials were to exert any authority in the frontier zone, they had to work with and not against the wishes of the *trekboers*.

It is sometimes asserted that these embryonic Afrikaners were a Puritan community, comparable with their contemporaries in New England.[28] Nothing could be further from the truth. With the exception of fewer than two hundred French Huguenots, who arrived in 1679–80, most of the original settlers were former employees of the Dutch East India Company and by no means particularly religious. The company treated the Dutch Reformed Church as the state church and appointed a few clergy to the Cape, but the religious establishment was no stronger than the lay bureaucracy.[29] *Trekboers* rarely encountered clergy, nor did they possess the institutions of an organized Puritan community.

Family autonomy and slender economic, cultural, and political links with Cape Town and the world beyond were therefore the hallmarks of white frontier society in its formative period in South Africa. The fragility and yet the necessity of these links were demonstrated in 1795–1801, when *trekboer* factions ousted unpopular *landdrosts* from both Graaff-Reinet and Swellendam and proclaimed independent republics. They proved incapable of creating effective political institutions or acquiring general legitimacy in their own communities, so the Cape authorities brought them to heel by cutting off ammunition supplies.[30]

The British regime transformed the institutions of local government in the Cape Colony, but the voortrekkers revived them in their republics. Elected *veldkornets* played important roles at the local level, especially in dealings with Africans.[31] At the state level, however, the voortrekkers were endemically factious. They migrated from the Cape Colony in numerous compact groups of kinsmen and neighbors and founded their new homes in widely dispersed localities. Bitter rivalries developed among leaders of the principal groups. They differed about the policies they should adopt towards the British officials and the principles on which they should establish their own government. In Natal, their first, abortive republic, they tried to manage with an all-powerful elected legislature and no executive, but in practice Andries Pretorius emerged as an independent leader.[32] Those who settled in the Orange Free State eventually rallied behind a written constitution that established a balance between a unicameral, elected legislature (*volksraad*) and an elected president. The Orange Free State constitution contained several provisions taken from the American constitution: clauses proclaiming equality before the law, debarring the *volksraad* from prohibiting peaceful assembly and petition, and guaranteeing the right to property as well as personal freedom and freedom of the press subject to law. It also included an amending procedure that was much more difficult than the procedure required for ordinary legislation. After a turbulent beginning—a mob forced the first president out of office—the Free Staters operated these institutions with considerable success. Constraints on legislators and officials were generally respected, and towards the end of the century the country earned the applause of visitors such as James Bryce, the British constitutional lawyer.[33]

The voortrekkers who settled beyond the Vaal River failed to devise stable political institutions for many years. Even though all their leaders had accepted a constitutional document by 1860, they quarreled again during the ensuing decade. In 1877 the state was so fragile that a small British detachment was able to run up the Union Jack in Pretoria and dismiss the president and the *volksraad* without any physical resistance. However, British misrule soon evoked a patriotic response, and after they had regained their independence in 1881, the Transvaalers allowed Paul Kruger to become a strong president. He was able to ignore the prolix and confused constitutional document when it suited his purpose, even to the extent of dismissing a chief justice who contended that the *volksraad* was not enacting laws constitutionally and that they were therefore invalid.[34] Kruger dealt shrewdly with the peripheral frontier zones abutting on African chiefdoms and coped skillfully with the problems of the internal frontier zone around Johannesburg until eventually both republics were overwhelmed by superior British forces.

Thus, in the Transvaal during the nineteenth century the excessively individualistic qualities promoted by dispersed settlement and a near-subsistence economy were gradually overborne by a strong, autocratic president in response to pressures from within and without. Both the anarchic and the authoritarian tendencies would survive into the twentieth century. After the Second World War, the latter would prevail, and South Africa would diverge still further from all other societies created by colonization from northwestern Europe.

The Frontier and Racial Attitudes

In an important pioneer work first published in 1937, I. D. MacCrone contended that racism in South Africa was essentially a frontier product—and especially a product of the *trekboer*-Khoisan frontier in the eighteenth century. He characterized *trekboer* society as individualistic, masculine, violent, and prone to degeneracy, but held together by a common racial consciousness.[35] MacCrone's views have now been modified in several respects. Winthrop Jordan and others have demonstrated that racist tendencies were present in European culture before the time of Columbus and da Gama.[36] Martin Legassick and others have shown that such tendencies were confirmed and sharpened by the company officials as well as the settlers in Cape Town and its vicinity in the seventeenth century, and that racist behavior is as much the product of interests as of attitudes.[37]

The society that took shape in the arable belt of good winter rainfall in the seventeenth century was culturally heterogeneous and sharply stratified. Differences of status and wealth corresponded roughly, though not precisely, with the easily discernible physical differences between the white officials and settlers and the rest of the population. By contemporary European standards, the Khoikhoi inhabitants were physically unattractive and culturally unimpressive. Indeed, travelers' reports were making "Hottentot" a byword in Europe for the lowest type of the human species.

Moreover, although other elements in the colonial population possessed valuable artisan skills, nearly all of them were slaves or former slaves. The eighteenth-century *trekboers* were therefore a
fragment of a society where dark-skinned people of all sorts had
inferior status and were regarded as inferiors.[38] The *trekboers'* own
experiences with hunter-collectors and Khoikhoi herders accen-
tuated their racist proclivities.[39] Later, in a statement written to
justify the emigration of the voortrekkers, Piet Retief equated race
with class,[40] and throughout the rest of the nineteenth century racism was a potent factor in all frontier zones between Boers and
Africans.

Men always outnumbered women in *trekboer* and voortrekker
society, for males predominated among the fresh arrivals from the
southwest. Consequently there was much concubinage between Boer
men and Khoikhoi and African women. Most of the offspring of
such unions were brought up by their mothers and excluded from
membership in Boer society. In some cases they formed communities with Khoikhoi families who were retreating before the advancing *trekboer* frontiersmen rather than becoming incorporated as
clients. Such communities were known as Bastards and later as Griquas. They were treated differentially by whites, even though they
resembled *trekboers* in their mode of life and their culture. Race
was the principal determinant of status in frontier society in southern Africa.[41]

In the nineteenth century, these southern African attitudes were
by no means unique. Racism was becoming more and more deeply
embedded in the European consciousness, and similar circumstances were evoking similar responses wherever white people
penetrated into alien societies, as in Australia and North America.
The British immigrants who settled in the eastern part of the Cape
Colony and in Natal rapidly became negrophobic because, in addition, they felt threatened by the numerically superior Africans around
them. They had left Britain in response to advertisements that emphasized the attractions of life in South Africa and made no reference to dangers. Whites on both sides did not recruit many blacks
to fight for them when they went to war with each other, as they
did in 1881 and 1899. Even missionaries, with few exceptions, con-

sidered it desirable to subject African chiefdoms to white control on the ground that that was a necessary prelude to converting and civilizing them.

For their part, in the early stages of their contacts with whites, the native peoples of southern Africa had scarcely any sense of racial solidarity. Depending on the context, Africans identified with their age group or sex group, their kinsfolk, their neighborhood, their chiefdom, or, at most, their linguistic community. The Nguni (Xhosa, Zulu, Mpondo, and so on) perceived themselves as being different from the Sotho, and vice versa; both groups distinguished themselves from the Khoisan peoples. There were deep historic rivalries between chiefdoms and between different segments of the same chiefdom, and these were compounded by the *mfecane* wars, which caused such widespread material and moral collapse on the eve of the Great Trek that many Africans welcomed white missionaries, traders, government officials, and even voortrekkers as saviors. Indeed, the first reaction of most Africans to the arrival of white people was to try to incorporate them into their social and political systems and to enlist their support against their traditional rivals.[42] Survivors of an early-eighteenth-century shipwreck on the Mpondo coast became the progenitors of a clan still known as the Abelungu (white people).[43] Moshweshwe of Lesotho used missionaries as agents of territorial expansion as well as scribes and interpreters of the wider world, and, in his final effort to preserve autonomy for his people, he persuaded the British government to annex what was left of his country, rather than have it completely dismembered by the Boers of the Orange Free State.[44]

In most cases, crosscutting alliances were advantageous to whites. Whites had local allies in every significant frontier confrontation in southern Africa. In the seventeenth century, the Khoikhoi chiefdoms in the vicinity of the Cape peninsula split into supporters and opponents of the Dutch.[45] Khoikhoi and colored men fought on the side of the whites in the hundred years of intermittent warfare against the Xhosa and the Thembu; so, after 1835, did the Mfengu, people of northern Nguni origin who fled westwards from the Zulu and were placed by British officials on land conquered from the Xhosa.[46] Colored clients accompanied the voortrekkers and worked for them and fought for them; thirty colored men died with Piet Retief and seventy other white voortrekkers at the hands of the Zulu.[47] Mpande split the Zulu nation, and it was his regiments that delivered the final blow to Dingane in 1840.[48] Whites used Swazi allies in their campaigns against the Pedi in the eastern Transvaal.[49] African contingents recruited in the colony of Natal fought alongside the British army against the Zulu in 1879 and alongside the Natal militia against the rebel forces in 1906.[50] And so on, through every frontier campaign in southern Africa; the converse, however, did not apply. Scarcely any whites helped Africans resist white expansion. Even John Dunn, a Scottish adventurer whom the Zulu monarchy provided with wives, cattle, and chiefly status, deserted to the British directly after the war began in 1879.[51]

An image of Africans as savages has persisted to this day. A sculpted frieze around the inside wall of the monument that was built on a hill overlooking Pretoria to celebrate the centenary of the Great Trek commemorates the death of Piet Retief and his party at the hands of the Zulu and the subsequent voortrekker victory at "Blood River."

Land, Labor, and the Seeds of Apartheid

By the seventeenth century there were vast differences between the economic and cultural institutions that existed in northwestern Europe—and especially in the Low Countries—and those that prevailed elsewhere. In northwestern Europe, land was owned by private individuals and was disposable by sale and testament, like other commodities. In southern Africa, on the other hand, land was regarded as being, in the last resort, the property of the community. Its use for hunting, collecting, and pasturage was also communal, but among arable farmers each household had the exclusive use of specific portions of land during the cultivating season. A chief, in consultation with his councillors, could admit newcomers into the chiefdom and grant them the same rights as those of existing members, but he could also revoke the rights of a person who abused them—for instance, by failing to cultivate his fields or by disloyal behavior.

Second, in northwestern Europe wage labor was already an established practice; indeed, most of the men who became settlers in South Africa in the seventeenth and eighteenth centuries did so after a period of service in the Dutch East India Company. Moreover, slavery was an established institution in the rest of the Dutch empire by the time the Cape settlement was founded, and the company imported slaves into the Cape Colony soon afterwards. Among southern African indigenous societies, on the other hand, there was no money economy and no wage labor, and the various forms of clientage and of communal labor for a chief fell far short of slavery. The most inferior person was not a chattel.

Third, for most of the inhabitants of northwestern Europe, cultural transmission was predominantly an informal process that took place within the home, supplemented in various degrees and with various effects by the teachings of religious authorities and the discipline imposed by employers. These practices promoted individualism and differentiation. Standardized public education was the exception rather than the rule in Europe before the late nineteenth century. Among southern Africans, on the other hand, early transmission within the family was followed by about six months of intensive formal education under the control of elders, who inculcated the norms of the society to boys and girls in separate initiation schools—a process that included rituals that emphasized the passage from adolescence to maturity and promoted social solidarity.[52]

When Europeans encountered Africans, differences such as these were compounded by communication problems. Their languages were poles apart, and the meanings of words were often distorted in translation, so even when both parties were negotiating in good faith, there was scope for serious misunderstanding. An African chief such as Moshweshwe might construe an agreement as meaning that he was permitting a white family to occupy a designated piece of land on customary African conditions, whereas the family in question might genuinely believe that they had bought the land and could do with it whatever they wished. Often, however, white settlers did not act in good faith but raised their expectations and stepped up their demands as their power in a frontier zone increased.

As the southern African frontiers advanced, the whites devised policies to reconcile their conflicting interests. For reasons of security and economy, colonial governments, as we have seen, tried repeatedly to prevent frontier zones from coming into being by proclaiming boundaries and prohibiting all forms of intercourse between the colonial and the indigenous societies. But we have also seen that such attempts were of no avail. From the very beginning, white settlers in southern Africa ignored the boundaries and used indigenous people as well as imported slaves as laborers. These contradictory tendencies—exclusive and incorporative—have persisted to the present day in southern Africa; so has the synthesis that emerged in the frontier era. Settlers sought to acquire the services of as many indigenous people as they needed but to exclude all other Africans from the lands they claimed as farms.

Natal is a good example of this process. While it was a voortrekker republic, the territory was still an open frontier zone, and physical force was the principal mode of interaction. The voortrekkers needed more servants than the colored people they had brought with them from the Cape Colony, and they turned to the local population. At first, as a result of the *mfecane* wars, there were few Africans in the area claimed by the voortrekkers, so the commandos that fought against the Zulu made a point of capturing children as well as cattle for distribution when a campaign ended. The captives were called apprentices and were meant to become free at the age of twenty-one, if male, or twenty-five in the case of females. However, from the Blood River campaign onward there was a continuous influx of Africans into Natal—people who were returning to homelands from which they had been ejected by Shaka two decades earlier. It has been estimated that the African population of the Natal Republic increased from ten thousand in 1838 to fifty thousand in 1843. Consequently the voortrekkers had reason to be concerned about the threat to their security. To cope with this problem, the Natal *volksraad* decided that no more than five African families should live on one farm, and it passed laws prohibiting Africans from owning firearms or horses, denying Africans the right to exist in the white areas of the republic except as servants of white people, and requiring Africans who were there to possess passes signed by their employers when they left their employers' property. In 1843 the *volksraad* also resolved that all "surplus" Africans should be moved southward beyond the Mtamvuna River, and it instructed the commandant-general to send them there, by persuasion if possible and by force if necessary. But that was never done. More and more Africans lived in the republic, and they were not effectively controlled by the white authorities. The voortrekker state was too weak to enforce its blueprint.[53]

After the British annexation of Natal, the colonial government faced the same problem of reconciling the need for security with the labor demands of settlers. The African population continued to mount rapidly as people returned both from kwa-Zulu across the Tugela River to the north and from Mpondo country to the south. By 1870 the colony contained about a quarter of a million Africans and only eighteen thousand whites, most of whom were recent immigrants from Britain. It was Theophilus Shepstone, a colonial-born son of a missionary, who, as secretary for native affairs, masterminded the solution to the problem. In so doing, he was obliged to pay serious attention to the interests of the settlers, who acquired a major say in affairs with the introduction of a representative form of government in 1856. He supervised the movement of most of the Africans to reservations (known locally as "locations"), where they were able to maintain their traditional customs and mode of production, but with important modifications. Their chiefs were subordinated to white officials. Their disputes with whites were adjudicated by magistrates, who applied the Roman Dutch law of the colony. The Africans paid an annual tax for every hut they occupied, and they were exposed to new commodities and new ideas by white traders and missionaries. The remaining Africans were occupants of mission reserves; squatters on crown lands; rent-paying residents on land owned but not occupied by white people, including commercial companies that derived substantial earnings from this practice of "kaffir-farming"; or farm laborers, paid partly in cash but largely in kind.[54]

This arrangement was in essence an application of the principal expedients that the voortrekker government had envisaged but lacked the means to enforce. Initially, although the white settlers got possession of most of the land, including most of the fertile land, the reservations were sufficient to sustain the bulk of the African population, and some Africans even managed to produce a surplus of grain for sale to whites. By the end of the century, however, the Africans had increased to over half a million, and they still outnumbered the whites by ten to one, yet the whites owned nearly four-fifths of the land, while the reservations amounted to less than one-fifth and were overcrowded, deteriorating, and net importers of food. The result was that about half the African population did not live in the reservations but on private lands belonging to white people. By working for whites the Africans tried to make up the difference between what they produced and what they needed for subsistence, for tax payments, and in some cases for rent. Except for the farm laborers, a typical African family sent one or more of its members for a year or so at a time to the towns and villages in Natal, to railroad construction sites, to the Kimberley diamond fields, or to the gold-mining industry on the Witwatersrand. There, African wages were extremely low. The majority of the whites knew scarcely anything about the conditions in the reservations and accepted the myth that African earnings supplemented a prosperous subsistence economy. Thus, by the time the frontier era closed, the African population of Natal was poverty-ridden. Migrant labor had become a necessity for Africans and a boon for whites. Some of the Africans rebelled against these conditions in 1906, but they were vigorously suppressed by the Natal militia.[55]

The process of African impoverishment in Natal was typical of the region as a whole. In other frontier zones whites gradually obtained possession of choice land and control of the labor they required. Initially they achieved their goals by the use of force, which was gradually superseded by bureaucratic controls.[56] There, too, however, was usually a period when the Africans were able to produce a surplus of grain, with a ready market among the white population.[57] On the high veld, for example, the Afrikaners were essentially a pastoral community until the end of the nineteenth century, as their predecessors had been in the Cape Colony in the eighteenth century. However, land losses plus population increase and taxation gradually turned the African reservations into importers of food and exporters of labor. The tempo of African incorporation into the white-controlled, capitalist economy increased rapidly after 1870. By 1899 the gold-mining industry possessed an elaborate labor recruiting organization, and cheap, black, migrant labor was a core feature of the political economy of the entire southern African region.[58]

Meanwhile, the indigenous peoples of southern Africa were becoming influenced, in various degrees, by western culture. As the Khoikhoi survivors became incorporated in the Cape Colony in the seventeenth and eighteenth centuries, they became an atomized rural and urban proletariat, adopting the culture of their masters. Christian missionaries were not a significant factor in southern Africa before the nineteenth century. Consequently, they had little effect on the white/Khoisan frontier during most of its existence, but from the beginning of the nineteenth century missionaries worked inside as well as outside the Cape Colony, and eventually almost the entire Cape colored community became Christian, with the exception of the descendants of some of the Asian slaves, who remained Muslim.

In the white/African frontier zones of the nineteenth century, however, European missionaries were the principal transmitters of the intrusive culture. Numerous British and continental missionary societies operated in the region, and in many frontier zones missionaries were the first white residents—the true pioneers—to be followed by traders and settlers. They often attached themselves to African chiefs and served as communicators with white secular authorities and informants about the wider world. Among the Mfengu and the Basotho, whose societies had been disrupted by the *mfecane* wars, they soon made converts, for the traditional rituals and belief systems had already proved incapable of averting disaster. Generally, however, extensive conversions were delayed until whites had established hegemony over a zone. Then, Africans looked to missionaries as people who had access to powers that would help them cope with a situation their ancestors had never envisaged. By the end of the nineteenth century, nearly all the African peoples of the region had experienced missionary influence, at least secondhand, and nearly a quarter of them had been baptized into a mission church.[59]

The missionaries have been judged in different ways. They have been applauded as beneficent advisors, modernizers, and mediators between the two cultures, as well as evangelists.[60] They have also been denounced as agents in conquest.[61] In fact, missionaries varied greatly. Some, such as Eugene Casalis, the first French Protestant missionary to Moshweshwe of Lesotho, identified closely with the people among whom they worked. Others identified essentially with white settlers, as did several of the Wesleyan missionaries to the Xhosa.

Since missionaries founded the first schools for Africans and provided nearly all the western education that was available to them in the nineteenth century, their influence over the first generations of literate Africans was profound. However, while they often criticized the discriminatory laws and practices of white society, even the most sensitive missionaries were firmly grounded in nineteenth-century European culture. They believed it was their duty to civilize as well as to evangelize, and their model of civilization was an idealized version of contemporary Europe. Consequently, they denounced customs that were integral to the cohesion and stability of African societies, including bride-price, polygyny, clientage, and traditional educational systems, and thereby alienated their proteges from their own backgrounds, including, in many cases, their own families.[62]

Missionaries also transmitted their own political attitudes, arousing expectations that colonial society was capable of fundamental reform, including the incorporation of Africans into full citizenship. This approach found no encouragement in the Boer republics, which applied absolute, all-pervasive color bars, and very little encouragement in Natal, but in the Cape Colony the Constitution of 1853 provided that men could vote in parliamentary elections regardless of their race, provided they possessed specific economic and educational qualifications. By 1909, colored men amounted to 10 percent of the colonial electorate, and nearly 5 percent were Africans. Consequently, the new mission-educated African elite focused its attention on the Cape Colony, with the hope that the Cape System would be reformed and extended throughout southern Africa.[63] At the turn of the century, the British encouraged such hopes in the propaganda they produced to vindicate the war against the Boer republics, but disillusionment followed. The Treaty of Vereeniging that ended the war assured the Boers that no African would have the vote when parliamentary institutions were introduced in the former republics. The British government fulfilled that promise in 1907, and the constitution that united South Africa in 1910 created an all-white, sovereign central parliament.[64]

Thus, when the frontier era ended, the seeds of apartheid were already planted in southern Africa.

Some Comparisons with the Frontier in North America[65]

The southern African frontier is comparable with the North American. Both are regional examples of frontiers created by the expansion of Europe and of the market economy in the modern era. In both cases there was a vast technological gulf between the intruders, who had access to firearms, wheeled transport, and a literary culture, and the indigenous peoples, who previously possessed none of those things. In both cases the intruders were predominantly settlers, committed to creating permanent homes for themselves and their descendants in the successive frontier zones. The vast majority of the settlers in both regions came from the Protestant culture of northwestern Europe. And in both regions settlers acquired political autonomy before the frontiers finally closed and were largely responsible for prescribing the status and the role of the surviving indigenous peoples. Nevertheless, there were enormous differences between the frontier processes in the two regions and, consequently, between the structures of the two societies that emerged from the frontier epoch at the end of the nineteenth century.

The most crucial difference was numerical. By the time of Columbus, the inhabitants of the Americas had been isolated from the Eurasian landmass for many millennia, with the result that they had not experienced several of the diseases that were endemic in Europe. Consequently, the American Indians had no immunity against those diseases, and smallpox, in particular, caused catastrophe after catastrophe as it spread from the European fishing fleets in the Newfoundland banks and the Saint Lawrence estuary and from the Spanish settlements in the Caribbean and on the mainland. Throughout North America the disease frontier preceded the frontier of settlement; nearly every Indian community sustained losses that undermined its morale and damaged its social system as well as drastically reducing its numbers before it had to face European settlers.[66] Thereafter the settlers, with their access to superior technology, were able to acquire control over the land with relative ease.[67] In the western part of southern Africa the Khoisan peoples, too, were an isolated population, and they, too, suffered severely from smallpox. But the Bantu-speaking Africans of the eastern part of the region constituted the southernmost extension of the Eurasian population continuum. They were already conditioned to the diseases carried by Europeans, and smallpox epidemics do not seem to have affected them much more severely than those outbreaks affected the white settlers.

Furthermore, the scale of European migration to the two regions differed immensely. North America had the natural resources to attract large numbers of Europeans from the seventeenth century onward, whereas southern Africa provided scarcely any attraction before the 1870s, and even then the influx was minute in comparison with the flood that flowed westward across the Atlantic. Consequently, North American settlers were soon able to muster a majority in nearly every frontier zone in which they had a stake. When the frontiers closed at the end of the nineteenth century, Indians numbered only one-quarter of a million, or less than one-third of 1 percent of the population of the region, and their societies had been profoundly disrupted.[68] To the contrary, Africans outnumbered whites in all frontier zones in the eastern part of southern Africa, and, when the frontier epoch ended, they amounted to six million people, or 80 percent of the population of the southern African region. Their social systems remained substantially intact and vigorous despite their subjection to white hegemony.

Second, although the frontiers in both regions were parts of a single economic process, which Walter Prescott Webb and Immanuel Wallerstein have described from opposite ideological viewpoints,[69] they were so in different degrees. In North America every frontier zone was closely integrated into the market economy.[70] From an early stage the English colonies were providing their metropole with furs, timber, and tobacco, rice, and indigo, and at all subsequent stages, as the frontiers moved westward from the Atlantic seaboard, American frontiersmen were producing commodities for metropolitan markets. In southern Africa, on the other hand, the *trekboers* and voortrekkers were intentionally minimizing their dependence on the market, since it was controlled in the eighteenth century by a commercial company that exploited them and in the nineteenth century by a government that was alien and unsympathetic. Although the Boers required imported weaponry and, when possible, clothing and groceries, the cattle, sheep, and farm produce they gave in exchange did not reach Europe and were of relatively little indirect significance to the metropolitan economies. Thus, the American frontier economy was substantially capitalist and bred a tradition of successful acquisitiveness, whereas the southern African frontier economy was near the subsistence end of the spectrum, and the Boers were suspicious of the forces that controlled their overseas trade. Consequently, the Afrikaner people entered into a prolonged crisis when the closing of their frontiers coincided with the rise of the mining industries that led, for the first time, to the full integration of southern Africa into the capitalist world economy.[71] On the other hand, Americans, being full-blooded capitalists already, were able to adapt to the conditions created by the closing of their frontiers with comparative ease.

A third great difference between the frontier processes in the two regions concerns the fate of the indigenous peoples. In southern Africa, as we have seen, the frontier zones were scenes of economic integration. At all stages the whites depended on the labor services of the local inhabitants—first the Khoikhoi and later the Bantu-speaking Africans. By the end of the frontier epoch the Africans had become an original type of semiproletariat, supplying an oscillating flow of migrant labor to the white-controlled economy, since they could not wrest a full subsistence from their reservations. In North America, Indians and whites were partners in the fur trade, but that trade ceased in area after area as the game became exterminated. Indians did not perform other significant roles in the burgeoning capitalist economy in North America. Of the two main systems of production in the English colonies, one comprised self-sufficient settler communities and the other included slaves imported from Africa, and successive waves of European immigrants supplied the wage labor in the growing industrial sector in the nineteenth century. The Indians of North America who survived smallpox, wars, and removals ended up on reservations constituting a minute proportion of the continent they had formerly dominated and, since the whites had no use for them, were ignored until after the beginning of the twentieth century. Thus, the southern Africa that emerged from the frontier epoch was a *herrenvolk* democracy in which Africans formed a subordinate caste, whereas in North America surviving descendants of the indigenous inhabitants were excluded from the society created by the intruders who had displaced them.

NOTES

1. Frederick Jackson Turner, "The Significance of the Frontier in American History," *Annual Report of the American Historical Association for the Year 1893*, pp. 199–207.

2. Ray Allen Billington, *America's Frontier Heritage* (New York, 1966); *The American Frontier Thesis: Attack and Defense*, American Historical Association Pamphlet No. 101 (Washington, D.C., 1971); *Frederick Jackson Turner: Historian, Scholar, Teacher* (New York, 1973); and *Westward Expansion*, 4th ed. (New York, 1974). For Billington's view that the North American frontier was unique, see his essay "Frontiers," in *The Comparative Approach to American History*, ed. C. Van Woodward (New York, 1968), p. 76.

3. David Harry Miller and Jerome O. Steffen, eds., *The Frontier: Comparative Studies* (Norman, Okla., 1977); University of Oklahoma, *Comparative Frontier Studies: An Inter-Disciplinary Newletter*, Fall, 1975, ff.

4. New Haven, 1981.

5. Walter Prescott Webb, *The Great Plains* (Boston, 1931); and *The Great Frontier* (Boston, 1952).

6. Some of the above ideas about comparative frontier history are present in W. K. Hancock, "Perspective View," in *Survey of British Commonwealth Affairs*, vol. II, *Problems of Economic Policy, 1918–1939*, part 1 (London, 1940), pp. 1–72; Marvin W. Mikesell, "Comparative Studies in Frontier History," *Annals of the American Academy of Political and Social Science*, March, 1960, pp. 62–74; Martin Legassick, "The Griqua, the Sotho-Rswana, and the Missionaries, 1780–1840: The Politics of a Frontier Zone," Ph.D. diss., University of California at Los Angeles, 1970, pp. 1–29, 634–68; John D. Forbes, "Frontiers in American History and the Role of the Frontier Historian," *Ethnohistory*, 16 (1968): 203–34; Robin F. Wells, "Frontier Systems as a Sociocultural Type," *Papers in Anthropology*, 14 (1973): 6–15; Jackson K. Putnam, "The Turner Thesis and the Westward Movement: A Reappraisal," *Western Historical Quarterly*, 7 (1976): 377–404; and Alastair Hennessy, *The Frontier in Latin American History* (Albuquerque, 1978). A somewhat more elaborate statement forms chapters 1 and 2 of Lamar and Thompson, *Frontier in History*.

7. John H. Wellington, *Southern Africa: A Geographical Study*, 2 vols. (Cambridge, 1955, 1960); F. J. Potgieter, "Die Vestiging van die Blanke in Transvaal, 1837–86," *Archives Year Book for South African History*, 1958, II (hereafter cited as *AYB*); N. C. Pollock and S. Agent, *An Historical Geography of South Africa* (London, 1964).

8. Summaries of the prehistory of southern Africa are in Leonard Thompson, ed., *African Societies in Southern Africa: Historical Studies* (London and New York, 1969); Monica Wilson and Leonard Thompson, eds., *The Oxford History of*

South Africa (Oxford, 1969) I, chapters 1–4 (hereafter cited as *OHSA*); Ray Ins-keep, *The Peopling of Southern Africa* (Cape Town, 1978); and D. W. Phillipson, *The Later Pre-history of Eastern and Southern Africa* (New York, 1978).

   9. Richard H. Elphick, *Kraal and Castle: Khoikhoi and the Founding of White South Africa* (New Haven, 1977); Shula Marks, "Khoisan Resistance to the Dutch in the Seventeenth and Eighteenth Centuries," *Journal of African History*, 13, no. 1 (1972): 55–80 (hereafter cited as *JAH*).

   10. On the *trekboers*, see L. Fouche, *Die evolutie van die trekboer*, (Pretoria, 1909); Eric A. Walker, *The Frontier Tradition in South Africa* (Oxford, 1930); P. J. van der Merwe, *Die noordwaartse beweging van die Boere voor die Groot Trek, 1770–1842*, (Cape Town, 1938); P. J. van der Merwe, *Trek: Studies oor die mobili-teit van die pioniersbevolking aan die Kaap* (Cape Town, 1945); J. S. Marais, *May-nier and the First Boer Republic* (Cape Town, 1944); S. D. Neumark, *Economic Influences on the South African Frontier, 1652–1836* (Stanford, Calif., 1957); W. K. Hancock, "Trek," *Economic History Review*, 10, no. 3 (1957–58): 331–39; Leonard Guelke, "Frontier Settlement in Early Dutch South Africa," *Annals of the Associa-tion of American Geographers*, 66, no. 1 (March, 1976): 25–42. The best eyewit-ness accounts of *trekboers* are Anders Sparrman, *Travels in the Cape, 1772–1776*, 2 vols. (London, 1785; Van Riebeeck Society edition, ed. Vernon S. Forbes, 1975, 1977); and Henry Lichtenstein, *Travels in Southern Africa in the Years 1803, 1804, 1805, 1806*, trans. from German by Anne Plumptre, 2 vols. (London, 1812, 1815; Van Riebeeck Society reprint, 1928, 1930).

   11. J. S. Marais, *The Cape Coloured People, 1652–1937*, 2d ed., (Johannes-burg, 1957); Shula Marks, "Khoisan Resistance." See also John B. Wright, *Bushmen Raiders in the Drakensberg, 1840–1870* (Pietermaritzburg, 1971), for a late stage of activity by aboriginal hunters-collectors in the Drakensberg Mountains and up-per Natal.

   12. Monica Wilson, "Co-operation and Conflict: The Eastern Cape Frontier," *OHSA*, I, ch. 6; W. M. Freund, "The Eastern Frontier of the Cape Colony during the Batavian Period (1803–1806)," *JAH*, 13, no. 4 (1972): 631–45; W. M. Freund, "Thoughts on the Study of the Cape Eastern Frontier Zone," in *Beyond the Cape Frontier*, ed. Christopher Saunders and Robin Derricourt (London, 1974), pp. 83–99; and Christopher Saunders, "The Hundred Years War: Some Reflections on Af-rican Resistance on the Cape-Xhosa Frontier," in *Profiles of Self-Determination*, ed. David Chanaiwa (Northridge, Calif., 1976). There is a contemporary account of the Xhosa on the eve of their first definitive defeat by an exceptionally perceptive Dutch official: *Ludwig Alberti's Account of the Tribal Life and Customs of the Xhosa in 1807*, trans. from German by William Fehr (Cape Town, 1968).

   13. C. F. J. Muller, *Die Oorsprong van die Groot Trek* (Cape Town, 1974).

   14. J. D. Omer-Cooper, *The Zulu Aftermath: A Nineteenth-Century Revolu-tion in Bantu Africa* (Evanston, Ill., 1966). There is an excellent contemporary description of the situation on the high veld on the eve of the Great Trek in William F. Lye, ed., *Andrew Smith's Journal of His Expedition into the Interior of South Africa, 1834–36* (Cape Town, 1975).

   15. Eric A. Walker, *The Great Trek*, 5th ed. (London, 1965), is still the best monograph on the Great Trek. See also my passages on pp. 355–73 and 405–24 of *OHSA*, I, and C. F. J. Muller, "The Period of the Great Trek, 1834–1854," in *Five Hundred Years: A History of South Africa*, ed. C. F. J. Muller (Pretoria, 1969), pp.

122–56. Contemporary accounts include William C. Harris, *The Wild Sports of Southern Africa*, 5th ed. (London, 1852); and documents in Edwin W. Smith, *The Life and Times of Daniel Lindley (1801–1880): Missionary to the Zulus, Pastor of the Voortrekkers* (London, 1949); and John Bird, ed., *The Annals of Natal: 1495–1845*, 2 vols. (Pietermaritzburg, 1888).

16. Leonard Thompson, *Survival in Two Worlds: Moshoeshoe of Lesotho* (Oxford, 1975); and Peter B. Sanders, *Moshoeshoe, Chief of the Sotho* (London, 1975).

17. Leonard Thompson, "The Subjection of the African Chiefdoms," in *OHSA*, II:244–86. African resistance has become a major theme in recent historical writing—for example, Chanaiwa, *Profiles of Self-Determination*.

18. The standard account of the Zulu war is Donald R. Morris, *The Washing of the Spears* (New York, 1965). Revisionist essays, sharply critical of the British, are John Wright, "Beyond the Washing of the Spears"; Jeff Guy, "The British Invasion of Zululand: Some Thoughts for the Centenary Year"; and Peter Colenbrander, "An Imperial High Commissioner and the Making of a War" in *Reality*, 11, no. 2 (Jan., 1979).

19. The following table, derived from the *Report of the Natives Land Commission, 1913–16, U.G. 19 (1916)*, I, app. 3, p. 9, and app. 4, p. 9, indicates the distribution of the land and of the "native" (that is, Bantu-speaking African) population in the Union of South Africa in about 1913, when the frontier era had closed:

	Urban areas	Farms owned by whites	Farms owned by whites but occupied by natives only	Native reserves, mission reserves, and farms owned by natives	Crown lands occupied by natives	Unoccupied Crown lands
The percentage of the total land area in different categories						
Cape Province	1.3	78.1	0.1	9.3	0.1	11.2
Natal	0.9	48.4	9.5	30.4	3.2	7.5
Transvaal	1.2	61.0	9.1	4.4	1.6	22.5
O.F.S.	1.4	97.0	0.0	1.5	0.0	0.0
The Union	1.2	74.0	2.9	8.9	0.7	12.4
The percentage of the total native population on the different categories of land						
Cape Province	8.0	15.0	0.5	75.7	0.8	
Natal	3.5	33.1	7.9	52.0	3.4	
Transvaal	23.3	29.6	16.8	25.1	5.2	
O.F.S.	14.0	79.4	0.0	6.6	0.0	
The Union	12.2	29.1	7.4	48.6	2.7	

20. J. S. Marais, *The Fall of Kruger's Republic* (Oxford, 1961); G. Blainey, "Lost Causes of the Jameson Raid," *Economic History Review*, 2d ser., 18 (1964–65): 350–66; R. V. Kubicek, "The Landlords in 1895: A Reassessment," *Journal of British Studies*, 11, no. 2 (1972): 84–103; Stanley Trapido, "The South African Republic: Class Formation and the State, 1850–1900," Institute of Commonwealth

Studies, London, *Collected Seminar Papers, Societies of Southern Africa*, vol. III (London, 1973): 57–65 (hereafter cited as ICS). Kimberley set a precedent for the organization of a mining industry in the 1870s; but the scale of the Witwatersrand gold mining industry rapidly surpassed Kimberley's diamond industry.

21. On the Dutch period, see A. J. "Böeseken in Muller, *Five Hundred Years*, pp. 16–63; M. F. Katzen, "White Settlers and the Origin of a New Society," in *OHSA*, I: 187–232; and Richard H. Elphick and Hermann Giliomee, *The Shaping of South African Society, 1652–1820* (Cape Town, 1979).

22. C. W. de Kiewiet, *British Colonial Policy and the South African Frontier, 1834–54* (Berkeley and Los Angeles, 1963).

23. C. W. de Kiewiet, *The Imperial Factor in South Africa: A Study in Politics and Economics* (Cambridge, 1937); Jean van der Poel, *The Jameson Raid* (Cape Town, 1951); Ronald Robinson and Jack Gallagher, with Alice Denny, *Africa and the Victorians: The Official Mind of Imperialism* (London, 1961); Jeffrey Butler, *The Liberal Party and the Jameson Raid* (London, 1968); Deryck Schreuder, *Gladstone and Kruger* (London, 1969); Anthony Atmore and Shula Marks, "The Imperial Factor in South Africa: Towards a Reassessment," *Journal of Imperial and Commonwealth History*, 3, no. 1 (1974).

24. G. Pyrah, *Imperial Policy and South Africa, 1902–1910* (Oxford, 1955); Leonard Thompson, *The Unification of South Africa, 1902–1910* (Oxford, 1960); W. K. Hancock, *Smuts*, vol. I, *The Sanguine Years, 1870–1919* (Cambridge, 1962); G. H. L. Le May, *British Supremacy in South Africa, 1899–1907* (Oxford, 1965); D. J. N. Denoon, *A Grand Illusion: The Failure of Imperial Policy in the Transvaal Colony during the Period of Reconstruction, 1900–1905* (London, 1973).

25. Opinions differ as to the extent to which *trekboer* society was involved in a market economy and capitalist in spirit. Neumark, in *Economic Influences*, contends that the frontier economy was fundamentally commercial; Guelke, in "Frontier Settlement," considers that it was essentially near subsistence. In "Social and Economic Processes on the South African Frontier," in Lamar and Thompson, *Frontier in History*, Robert Ross explains that (1) the *trekboers* produced most of their subsistence needs, (2) they were marginally in the orbit of the market and the money economy, and (3) they exploited commercial opportunities when they became available. I agree with Ross but would stress that their commercial opportunities were meager compared with those of most North American and Australian frontiersmen.

26. P. J. Venter, "Landdros en Heemrade (1682–1827)," *AYB*, 1940, II.

27. D. de Jongh, *Het krijgswezen onder de Oostindische Compagnie* (The Hague, 1950); G. Tylden, "The Development of the Commando System in South Africa, 1715 to 1922," *Africana Notes and News*, 13, no 8 (Dec., 1959): 303–13.

28. W. A. de Klerk, *The Puritans in Africa: A Story of Afrikanerdom* (Harmondsworth, 1975).

29. A. Moorrees, *Die Nederduitse Gereformeerde Kerk in Suid-Afrika, 1652–1873* (Cape Town, 1937); G. D. Scholtz, *Die geskiedenis van die Nederduitse Hervormde of Gereformeerde Kerk van Suid-Afrika*, 2 vols. (Cape Town, 1956, 1960).

30. J. S. Marais, *Maynier and the First Boer Republic* (Cape Town, 1944).

31. F. A. van Jaarsveld, "Die Veldkornet en sy aandeel in die opbou van die Suid-Afrikaanse Republiek tot 1870," *AYB*, 1950, II.

32. J. A. I. Agar-Hamilton, *The Native Policy of the Voortrekkers: An Essay in*

the History of the Interior of South Africa, 1836–1858 (Cape Town, 1928); A. J. du Plessis, "Die Republiek Natalia," *AYB*, 1942, I.

33. James Bryce, *Impressions of South Africa* (London, 1897), pp. 323–30; J. H. Malan, *Die opkoms van'n Republiek* (Bloemfontein, 1929); G. D. Scholtz, *Die Konstitutie en die Staatsinstellings van die Oranje-Vrijstaat* (Amsterdam, 1937); Leonard Thompson, "Constitutionalism in the South African Republics," *Butterworths South African Law Review*, 1954, pp. 50–72; J. M. Orpen, *Reminiscences of Life in South Africa* (Cape Town, 1964).

34. F. A. F. Wichman, "Die wordingsgeskiedenis van die Zuid-Afrikaansche Republiek, 1838–1860," *AYB*, 1941, II; J. S. du Plessis, "Die onstaan en ontwikkeling van die amp van die staatspresident in die Zuid-Afrikaansche Republiek (1858–1902)," *AYB*, 1955, I; D. W. Kruger, *Paul Kruger*, 2 vols. (Johannesburg, 1961, 1963); Thompson, "Constitutionalism."

35. I. D. MacCrone, *Race Attitudes in South Africa: Historical, Experimental and Psychological Studies* (London, 1937).

36. Winthrop Jordan, *White over Black* (Chapel Hill, N.C., 1968).

37. Martin Legassick, "The Frontier Tradition in South African Historiography," in *Economy and Society in Pre-industrial South Africa*, ed. Shula Marks and Anthony Atmore (London, 1980), pp. 44–79.

38. W. M. Freund, "Race in the Social Structure of South Africa, 1652–1936," *Race and Class*, 18, no. 1 (1976): 53–67; Elphick and Giliomee, *Shaping of South African Society.*

39. MacCrone includes ample evidence of this in *Race Attitudes*, chs. 6 and 7; so do the accounts of contemporaries such as Henry Lichtenstein, *Travels in Southern Africa*, and Anders Sparrman, *Travels in the Cape.*

40. G. W. Eybers, ed., *Select Constitutional Documents Illustrating South African History, 1795–1910* (London, 1918), pp. 143–45.

41. Robert Ross, *Adam Kok's Griquas: A Study in the Development of Stratification in South Africa* (Cambridge, 1976).

42. This is a central theme in Christopher Saunders, "Political Processes in the South African Frontier Zone," in Lamar and Thompson, *Frontier in History.*

43. Wilson, *OHSA*, I:233.

44. Thompson, *Survival in Two Worlds*, chs. 3 and 7.

45. Elphick, *Kraal and Castle*, pp. 130–31.

46. Wilson, *OHSA*, I:249.

47. Thompson, *OHSA*, I:360.

48. Ibid., p. 363.

49. C. J. Uys, *In the Era of Shepstone* (Lovedale, South Africa, 1933), p. 205.

50. Morris, *Washing of the Spears*; Shula Marks, *Reluctant Rebellion: The 1906–1908 Disturbances in Natal* (Oxford, 1970).

51. Thompson, *OHSA*, II:264.

52. For an example of the traditional initiation system, see my *Survival in Two Worlds*, pp. 3–5.

53. Agar-Hamilton, *Native Policy*; du Plessis, "Die Republiek"; Edgar H. Brookes and Colin de B. Webb, *A History of Natal* (Pietermaritzburg, 1965), pp. 29–41; Thompson, *OHSA*, I:364–68.

54. Brookes and Webb *History of Natal*, pp. 54–74; Smith, *Daniel Lindley*, pp. 250–303; David Welsh, *The Roots of Segregation: Native Policy in Colonial*

Natal, 1845–1910 (Cape Town, 1971); *OHSA*, I: 373–90; H. Slater, "Land, Power and Capital in Natal: The Natal Land and Colonization Company, 1860–1948," *JAH*, 16, no. 2 (1975):275–83.

55. Natal, *Natal Native Affairs Commission, 1906–7*, 2 vols. (Pietermaritzburg, 1907); Marks, *Reluctant Rebellion*.

56. For eyewitness accounts of the kidnapping of indigenous children in the 1850s, see Orpen, *Reminiscences of Life*, pp. 302–24.

57. Colin Bundy, "The Emergence and Decline of a South African Peasantry," *African Affairs*, 285 (1972):369–88.

58. Sheila T. van der Horst, *Native Labour in South Africa* (London, 1942); Robin Palmer and Neil Parsons, eds., *The Roots of Rural Poverty in Central and Southern Africa* (London, 1977).

59. The religious affiliations of the South African communities according to the 1911 census are summarized in Thompson, *Unification*, p. 488.

60. For example, see Brookes and Webb, *History of Natal*, pp. 101–102.

61. Nosipho Majeke, *The Role of the Missionaries in Conquest* (Johannesburg, 1952).

62. The Lesotho example is described in *Survival in Two Worlds*, ch. 3.

63. There is a useful collection of contemporaneous articles, written by missionaries and mission-educated Africans, in Francis Wilson and Dominique Perrot, eds., *Outlook on a Century: South Africa, 1870–1970* (Lovedale, 1973).

64. Thompson, *Unification*, pp. 109–26, 212–26, and 416–32.

65. The North American case is much more complex than the southern African. Here I highlight some of the most significant points of comparison with the frontiers created by the westward movement from the Atlantic Seaboard to the Pacific in what is now the United States, and, following Turner and Billington, I ignore the French, the Spanish, and the Mexican frontiers. The theme is developed at some length in Lamar and Thompson, *Frontier in History*. There is an elaborate bibliography on the history of the American frontier in Ray Allen Billington, *Westward Expansion: A History of the American Frontier*, 4th ed. (New York, 1974), pp. 663–805. See also Howard R. Lamar, ed., *The Reader's Encyclopedia of the American West* (New York, 1977).

66. Alfred W. Crosby, *The Columbian Exchange: Biological and Cultural Consequences of 1492* (Westport, Conn., 1972).

67. Francis Jennings, *The Invasion of America: Indians, Colonialism, and the Cant of Conquest* (Chapel Hill, 1975).

68. The number of other Americans who have at least one Indian American ancestor is not known; it may be considerable.

69. Immanuel Wallerstein, *The Capitalist World-Economy* (Cambridge, 1979).

70. David M. Potter, *People of Plenty: Economic Abundance and the American Character* (Chicago, 1954).

71. Hermann Giliomee, "The South African Frontier: Stages in Development," in Lamar and Thompson, *Frontier in History*.

Australia, the Frontier, and the Tyranny of Distance

WHEN Walter Prescott Webb published his interpretive volume *The Great Frontier* in 1952,[1] he made two of his pedagogical biases quite clear. He felt that the professional historian had an obligation to reach out to the "lay audience" (terminology which suggests that the professional historian sees himself as akin to the priest, the possessor of truth and wisdom, or at the least as a father confessor to the rest of society), to make history more than a matter of dancing on heads of pins. The heart of his book had already appeared in *Harper's* magazine and had caught the attention of many readers, including me in my senior year at college. Running through all of Webb's work was his conviction that what the historian had to say should count, should reach an enlarged audience, and might therefore need to be expressed in the terms of the essayist, the rhetorician, and the evangelist.

The Great Frontier breathed new life into the vision of Frederick Jackson Turner—a vision that not only accounted for America's uniqueness but also posited that uniqueness virtually as a mathematical given. Turner had not sought to demonstrate that the history of the United States was unique, or even exceptional; he had assumed this to be so and set out to account for why it was so. Webb was well aware that a body of scholars (most particularly Fred A. Shannon) were said to have driven the last nail into Turner's coffin by the 1930s, in the sense that they had proven him to be wrong on any number of factual points, inconsistent in any number of statements, and given to flights of poetry when good rock-hard social science analysis was called for. Yet while Webb conceded that Turner's explanations for American uniqueness had been seriously damaged, he also realized that virtually no one had questioned Turner's unspoken assumption that America *was* unique. That is, the answers had been "proven" wrong (in the sense that anything is "proven wrong" in history) while the question as asked was allowed to stand. Webb sought a broader answer which would let Turner's insights survive, or reassert themselves, by lengthening Turner's shadow.

Webb's second pedagogical bias was that since the New World had proved to be a great frontier to Europe, as he sought to demonstrate, then Europeans and especially European scholars should be interested in American history. He did not suggest that his American colleagues should examine frontiers elsewhere, with the possible result that they might find their own history somewhat less exceptional; rather, he was clearly disappointed that European historians had not sought to apply the Turnerian mode of analysis themselves. Let Webb speak for himself:[2]

> I have often thought that each nation has something peculiar to itself that could be borrowed with advantage by its neighbors. If I could export one thing American to European scholars, something which, I believe, would help them to a better understanding of their troubled world, our troubled world, it would be an understanding of the frontier—not the American frontier, but their own—and its significance in their history and in their present lives. . . . The basic assumption for the discussion of the frontier as a factor in western European civilization is that Europe, too, had a frontier.

He went on to elaborate his theory of world frontiers.

Although Webb's earlier book, *The Great Plains*, had placed heavy emphasis on material culture, on technology and artifactual change, *The Great Frontier* sought not only to widen the horizon but also to broaden the debate. He sought, as J. H. Elliott has noted, "to provide a comprehensive interpretation of modern history in terms of the New World and its impact on Europe."[3] He applied Turner to Europe, for which the whole of North America was one grand frontier. The opening of the New World to exploitation and settlement changed the ratio between land, population, and capital to create boom conditions in Europe. What had become a stable population in Europe now might enjoy a surplus of land and capital; this surplus led to four hundred years of boom, from 1500 to 1900. Precious metals and American produce were windfalls for Europe, providing the impetus to European capitalism, which, in turn, was sustained by secondary windfalls. The stimulation of bullion, of new trade and trade routes, and of visions and the reality of opportunity, provided Europe, the world we now refer to as simply the West, with its modern dynamism. Social mobility, land use, and institutional change were the proper subjects of study.

Webb's courageous, if not to say outrageous, book roamed the world as we might roam an encyclopedia, eager for knowledge of "many wonderful things." He commented on Africa, Brazil, British Guiana; on both the Dutch and the British East India companies; on Mexico, the West Indies, and the Republic of Texas; and on Canada, Australia, New Zealand, and South Africa. (Oddly, he did not comment on the Soviet Union or China.) He cited numerous popular articles, again testimony to his belief that the lay reader was important, from *Reader's Digest*, the *American Magazine*, and the *Saturday Evening Post*, all with the word "frontier" in their titles, and he appeared to endorse such usage, as when he referred to Ethiopia as the "Land of the Fabulous Frontier." He thereupon drew back to make it clear that he did not agree with hunting out frontiers in this manner; rather, he was examining, somewhat impressionistically, the evocative power of the word itself.

Two problems arise immediately. One arises from the tendency of historians who examine a concept derived from popular culture, especially when they feel that the concept to have essential validity, to put little or no explicit distance between themselves and the popular manifestations of the idea they are examining. Said differently, Frederick Jackson Turner knew that the frontier was both a place and a process, for he said so, but he also knew that it was a state of mind, and a state of mind that might outlast both the place and the process. He was careless, however, about which of these three frontiers he held in his own mind at a given moment, so his readers may be excused for occasional confusion. While Webb recognized this confusion in Turner, he, too, did not always separate that which could be factually demonstrated from that which "common sense", or what the historian's leap of faith from evidence to conclusion (or even strongly held personal wishes) might make true or clothe in the appearance of truth.

All historians who engage in what we somewhat loosely call social and intellectual history know perfectly well that they deal

with two truths simultaneously: the facts as the good, grey re-
searcher in us is able to verify them, and that which people believe
to be true. Webb respected the distinction, and like most historians
of his generation he felt his principal obligation was to the facts as
they could be reconstructed and proven; yet he was actually more
excited by the analyses of what people believe to be true which he
infiltrated (or, as the author of a book on the Texas Rangers may
have preferred, bootlegged) into his work. Today, I think, most historians would agree that if the historian's task is to interpret and
understand human motivation, it is far more important to know
what people believed to be true than to reconstruct the actual facts.
Webb was not in a position to concede this—hence his quite evident fascination with popular articles which helped to suggest that
Ethiopians, Canadians, and Australians all had much to learn from
Americans, coupled with his wry and deprecating remarks about
those articles.

What, in fact, did Australians, for example, have to learn from
The Great Frontier? Australia did not enter the picture until well
after the initial boom, and its history was to be fit into the concept
of the secondary windfall, when overseas societies helped to sustain
the capitalism already created. On this point there was some am-
bivalence, for by Webb's scheme secondary windfalls taken as a group
were not the creators of capitalism as such, and capitalism was, he
said, the product of the sixteenth and seventeenth centuries—that
is, long before Australia had been settled. Yet he included Australia
in his discussion of those primary windfalls which depended on the
"frontier treasure of gold and silver" while admitting that the settlement and exploitation of Australia fell outside the time-frame he
had imposed on the primary windfall.[4] This argument was less contradictory than it seemed, for he also provided specific verbal definitions of both types of windfalls even while clearly preferring his
functional definitions-by-usage. He referred to Australia in the context of the American cattle kings, asserting that "what happened in
the Great Plains also happened in South America, Australia, and
wherever grass grew on the free frontier."[5] He did not quote, though
he might well have, the words of Patrick Durack, who built an empire of cattle land in Australia of which he wrote in 1878, "'Cattle
Kings' ye call us, then we are Kings in grass castles that may be

PAPUA /
NEW GUINEA

• Darwin

NORTHERN

TERRITORY   QUEENSLAND

WESTERN

AUSTRALIA   SOUTH

AUSTRALIA   • Brisbane   NEW
                                                                ZEALAND
DARLING MTNS.
• Perth   Broken Hill •   NEW SOUTH
                                            WALES   • Auckland
                           Bathurst •   Blue Mtns
             • Adelaide   NORTH ISLAND
                                            • Sydney
                           Canberra •   (Port Jackson)
                        VICTORIA   • Wellington
             200 Mi.   • Melbourne   SOUTH ISLAND
                                                          • Christchurch

                        TASMANIA
                        (VAN DIEMEN'S • Hobart
                        LAND)

Australia in the Twentieth Century

blown away upon a puff of wind. . . ."[6] Webb referred only once more to Australia, when he was pleased to find that Turner's expectations, as they related to the law of primogeniture, proved relevant. But we will return to all of this shortly.

As to the second problem, arising from the manner in which Walter Prescott Webb chided European and other historians for not paying sufficient attention to American history and specifically to the contributions of Frederick Jackson Turner, there is little to say other than noting it. Webb remarked upon three scholars as exceptions who proved his case; two were Australians (one transplanted to England) and one was a South African teaching at Cambridge. One of these, the Australian W. K. (now Sir Keith) Hancock, had written of an Australian frontier in 1939 but admitted later that at the time he had never heard of Turner.[7] This tended to prove that European scholars were not paying sufficient attention to the lessons of American historiography. The real problem arises from the word "sufficient," for Webb was convinced of the relevance of the American experience to other experiences, and just as he showed signs of being annoyed when he felt that Texas was being ignored in the national historiography, he also transferred his sense of annoyance to the world scene. My point here is not that he was wrong, for he was not, but that he was allowing a tinge of pride, a hint of the emotional, to color his judgments. When his essay appeared in its popular form in the October, 1951, *Harper's*, the magazine was festooned with a special wrapper, at least on the newsstands of Colorado, pointing out to me (and to others in that last semester in college) that our state of Colorado had at last been shown to be relevant to—even, the wrapper hinted, at the center of—an understanding of the world. The cry that knowing us better would help Europeans to better understand themselves, while not so obviously commercial, was a sophisticated extension of the longing of all of us to step beyond ourselves, to be taken seriously, to be seen in our original worth. By the 1970s we had, perhaps, come full circle. We then became aware that scholars from Japan, the United Kingdom, or Australia, to mention three countries where one may say that the study of America came of age by the 1960s, had their own reasons for examining the United States, that these reasons were not to be dismissed as minor modifications of America's own

reasons for self-study, and that one must set the study of America
that originated abroad in the context of the culture from which the
study emerged. Americans may at last have accepted the fact that
other people study us for their, not for our, reasons.[8] This was precisely Webb's point yet, paradoxically, not his purpose.

Australians might well have wished to examine themselves in
order to free their historiography from European, and specifically
British, formulations. Most were unlikely to be willing to accept
American formulations any more readily, however, unless by doing
so they could liberate themselves from the greater danger. While
there were early Turnerians in Australia, their impact was small. It
was not until 1958 that a truly Australian view on the idea of an
Australian frontier was fully formulated, in this case by Russel Ward
in his book *The Australian Legend*.[9] The title he chose, while apparently misunderstood by some of his critics, may have derived
from the second and less clearly stated of Webb's concerns—that
with what people believed to be true. Still, Ward's book bore most
unmistakably the stamp not of Webb nor of Turner but of another
contributor to the continuum, Henry Nash Smith, who in *Virgin
Land: The American West as Symbol and Myth* breathed new life
into the old questions.[10]

And yet, and yet. . . . Just as Professor Hancock had reached
conclusions which were to be labeled Turnerian when, as he admitted, he had never heard of Turner, Russel Ward had written an
Australian *Virgin Land* without having ever read Smith's book. Australia had produced its own frontier thesis, or indeed theses, spon-
taneously. Distance had so tyrannized Australian scholarship that it
had forced Australian scholars to generate their own explanations
for how they came to be what they were. Just as Turner was delighted to find an explanation which not only would account for
American uniqueness but also would sever American historiography from European theorizing about the Teutonic forest or long-
dead barons at Runnymede, and just as Webb was pleased to reverse the flow and show that American historiography could, or at
least ought, to lay its hand upon the Europeans, the Australians
were delighted to escape from the conventional wisdoms in which
their earlier, largely imperial, historiography had them embedded.

What were these conventional wisdoms? Two are particularly

important here. The first was obvious and comprehensive: the tendency to write the history of Australia, indeed of all settler societies within the British Empire, in terms of an almost foreordained movement from colony to nationhood. Australian history was a subset within British colonial and imperial history. Constitutionally viewed, it appeared to be about the transfer of the common law, the English language, and other hallmarks of an empire in which, by stately steps, the Australian people were slowly moving, via the prescribed stages of representative and later responsible government, toward political independence.[11] Australian history was not only written as though from abroad. It was also an outward extension of a larger story, the basic outlines of which were determined abroad. Such a state of intellectual affairs was not likely to remain palatable in the 1950s, when Australians had discovered that at a stroke they had passed from the British to the American defensive umbrella, and when Australians were, in the face of an unprecedented immigration, trying to define what unique values they might have gained or retained from Britain.[12]

The second conventional wisdom arose from what is frequently called "open space theory"—that body of writing devoted to examining the ways in which various settler, or encroaching, peoples moved into spaces and onto land that was deemed "open" or "unsettled"—writing which tended to ignore the presence of indigenous populations. Turner's work was a contribution to this body of literature; so too was Webb's and James C. Malin's and S. Daniel Neumark's and P. J. van der Merwe's on South Africa and Harold A. Innis's on Canada. Louis Hartz would make a fundamental contribution to this body of theory in his work, *The Founding of New Societies*, in 1964.[13]

The prevailing expression of "open space theory" in the period when Australians sought, first, to apply their own frontier analysis to themselves and, second, to establish an independent line on the analysis was not that of Turner but of Sir Halford John Mackinder who read his influential paper, "The Geographical Pivot of History," to the Royal Geographical Society in London in January, 1904. That paper he expanded in 1919 as the book *Democratic Ideals and Reality*.[14] Mackinder was the first writer of major stature to apply the theory of closed space to the world, as suggested by Turner when he declared the frontier to have ended. The Columbian epoch of exploration and expansion was over, the path of progress once cut by the missionary, the conqueror, the farmer, and the miner was now to be built by the engineer. "Every shock, every disaster or superfluity, is now felt even to the antipodes, and may indeed return from the antipodes."[15] Here was a technocratic restatement of Macauley's Maori, an assertion of One World based on technology, which could and did appeal to the best Liberal-Imperialist, or, in the United States, to a Wendell Willkie and a Henry A. Wallace alike. There were four arcs which made the circle of commerce complete (a deliberate echo of an earlier mercantilist reasoning): the arcs of power, trade, wages, and labor. Here were population, land, and capital; there were bullion, trade, and opportunity. Mackinder had anticipated Webb clearly enough when he wrote, in his address, that "In 400 years the outline of the map of the world has been completed with approximate accuracy. . . ."[16] The frontier had vanished; the world would once again have to deal with a closed political system; four hundred years of boom were at an end.

Let me pause to say that just as Mackinder, however similar his ideas were to Turner's, did not cite Turner, so too Webb, however, similar he was in primary thrust to Mackinder, did not cite the Oxford geographer. Indeed, Mackinder appears in neither bibliography nor index to *The Great Frontier*. By noting the remarkable similarity of ideas here I do not mean to imply a borrowing, acknowledged or otherwise; rather, I mean to add weight to my contention that more than one scholar may arrive at the same or at least similar conclusions from the same data—stated this way it would be surprising if they did not—and that Webb's fretful concern that Europeans had yet to discover the frontier was simply wrong on two counts: in the person of Mackinder the Europeans already had discovered it, and, rather than applying it more directly as a result of reading American historians, they would come to their own frontier theses—theses arising from their own needs—when they were ready to.*

*In discussion following the presentation of the 1979 Webb lectures, several people wished to follow up on this point. Some remarked that it was not surprising that Webb did not acknowledge Mackinder, for he well might not have read him, or may have read him and deliberately chosen not to acknowledge him, as was his

Nor am I concerned here with the question of whether Webb
was correct—Elliott argues that he was not[17]—but rather I am
seeking to suggest why Australian scholars either should have embraced Turner and Webb (as in the instance of Fred Alexander,[18]
whom Webb singles out, or of Norman Harper)[19] or quite independently should have been seeking out their own applications of open
space theory. The latter group needed to escape from the kind of
geopolitics taught by Mackinder, adopted by Haushofer in Germany, and used by Nicolas Spykman in the United States. By the
late 1930s the Nazi Geopolitical Institute had borrowed so heavily
from Mackinder that to admit drawing upon his arguments was rather
like suggesting that Karl Marx was right while insisting one was not
a Marxist—a perfectly compatible intellectual position, though not
a tenable one in time of war. Even were the specter of justification
for *Lebensraum* not to hover over Mackinder, quite wrongly if for
the time irredeemably, Americans and Australians were unlikely to
embrace Mackinder's arguments (as they had, in fact, embraced
them early in the century) when those arguments kept the center
of attention squarely on Europe. Mackinder's view of Australia was

---

manner at times. Webb himself admitted that he saw little need for supplying footnotes to all of the materials he had consulted, since he would lose the larger audience he wished to reach (see his response to Fred Shannon's criticisms, as in note
24, below). He defended the sparing use of footnotes; see Walter Rundell, Jr.,
Walter Prescott Webb (Austin, 1971), p. 29. As is true of many fertile minds that
convert to their own purposes, and in fresh form, ideas which originally arose from
another source, Webb was at times likely to forget where an idea in a less sophisticated form first came from; see Necah Stewart Furman, *Walter Prescott Webb:
His Life and Impact* (Albuquerque, 1976), pp. 116 121. In any event, Webb first
thought of the theme which became *The Great Frontier* long before he wrote it,
while writing chapter six of *Divided We Stand*, which first appeared in 1937 (see
Furman, *Walter Prescott Webb*, p. 120). None of this detracts from Webb's origi-
nality, for the best scholarship knows how to assimilate ideas from others. In discussion it was suggested that Webb may not have mentioned Mackinder precisely
because he was a figure out of favor by World War II, when Webb—at Oxford
University in 1943—may have first encountered his work. Others speculated that
Arnold Toynbee's considerable influence on Webb (for the Texan admitted to much
admiring the Englishman) may have shut out other British influences. The specu-
lation is of little value in any event. I found the best approaches to Webb's strengths
and weaknesses in Larry McMurtry's *In a Narrow Grave: Essays on Texas* (New
York, 1968), which situates Webb amidst Teddy Blue, Roy Bedichek, and J. Frank
Dobie, and Gregory M. Tobin's perceptive inquiry, *The Making of a History: Walter Prescott Webb and* The Great Plains (Austin, 1976).

that it was decidedly on the periphery of events, and the New World was merely a satellite to the old continent; what mattered was dominance over the Heartland, the pivotal region of world politics, where the Natural Seats of Power might be found—that is, over Eurasia. As Mackinder hymned it, he who ruled Eastern Europe would command that Heartland; he who ruled the Heartland commanded the World-Island (which was Europe, Asia, and Africa, all linked by land), and he who ruled the World-Island commanded the World. In Europe this was the prevailing geopolitics of the period when Turner came under attack, and while the incredible development of air power under the pressures of World War II rendered Mackinder's map untenable, the imperial attitudes from which his view had arisen remained alive and well in Australian historiography.[20]

Yet in terms of the world scene, even in terms of British imperial history—the context into which an Oxford don was likely to fit Australia—or of open space theory, Mackinder's view that Australia was peripheral to the four hundred years of boom was right for his time. For a future time Mackinder was very wrong indeed, and one person who saw just how wrong he was going to be was another prophet of empire, R. S. Amery, who commented (in the discussion that took place at the Royal Geographical Society in 1904) that

> . . . both the sea and the railway are going in the future . . . to be supplemented by the air as a means of locomotion, and when we come to that . . . a great deal of this geography must lose its importance, and the successful powers will be those who have the greatest industrial base. It will not matter whether they are in the center of a continent or on an island; those people who have the industrial power and the power of invention and of science will be able to defeat all others.[21]

The Wright brothers had achieved the first powered flight exactly forty days before Mackinder spoke and Amery rebutted. It would be the effects of that flight, as much as the work of Australian historiographers, that would free the Australian frontier from the tyranny of distance.

Before turning back to Russel Ward's *The Australian Legend*, I must raise two more questions. In order to apply the insights of Turner or of Webb to other societies, historians must—it is said— engage in something called "comparative history"; why have they been so reluctant to do so? And in what way does another major contributor to frontier theory, Louis Hartz, speak to the problem of the Australian fragment, or expression, or European culture?

As W. Turrentine Jackson has remarked in one of his two superb articles on the notion of comparative frontiers,[22] historians have lagged behind scholars in other disciplines in their use of new methods of research by which they might arrive at comparative insights. Jackson points out that "of the two most often cited articles attempting to summarize the historical interpretations of comparative frontiers, one was written by a geographer and the other by a European specializing in American Studies." The persons referred to here are Marvin W. Mikesell and Dietrich Gerhard.[23] Jackson and others complain of this lack of comparative work, just as Webb did, while noting how many Australian scholars in particular have employed Turner in one way or another.[24] A word on comparative history thus seems in order.

For a long time, I think, universities in much of the world have made a mistake in organizing their history curricula around national identities.[25] Look to most university catalogs; there you will find courses called the History of the United States, the History of Germany, the History of France, the History of Canada, and (although remarkably seldom in the United States) the History of Australia. What such organization surely does (certainly for the less perceptive student) is to induce a subtle Whig bias by which students are led to believe that what history is all about is the rise of the nation-state. Thus one is studying history as a discipline primarily to learn why and how a particular nation came to be as it was and is. This conclusion in turn leads research students to the conclusion that the nation-state is the best receptacle for the collection of historical data.

Stated in this way, the contention is obviously false. The best receptacle for the collection of historical data clearly is not the nation-state. Lord Acton was right when he told us to study problems. If a problem is taken as the unit of study, however—that is, if one studies revolutions, not a revolution, studies imperialisms, not the imperialism of a single nation, studies frontiers, and not a frontier—then one is engaging, by the nature of things, in comparative history. This has the disadvantage of appearing to be merely fashionable to some. It has the very real disadvantage of being very difficult, requiring the scholar to break from the mold of single-language training and single-culture interpretations. It has the enormous disadvantage, in a world of those who perish when they do not publish, of being time-consuming and open to many potential dead ends. It tends to glibness. One will certainly be accused of superficiality. One may find that the end result is a kind of sophisticated parallel study instead of a comparative study. The charge of an inevitable superficiality is not untrue, yet inevitably what one does in national history is also superficial, and in ways more subtle and socially dangerous. None of these objections seem to me sufficient to set against the benefits of comparative work.

Still, there are two objections one must take most seriously. The first is that so often what one has done is to study the impact of one society upon another. Is this not what Walter Prescott Webb, in fact, did? And there is the objection that the comparative approach is restricted because it looks only at those problems capable of comparison. Surely this is true. That is to say, it is a mistake to compare the British Empire with the Roman Empire, a favorite game of the British themselves near the end of the nineteenth century—a game by which they could congratulate themselves and make foolish predictions about the length of time the empire would continue to grow. In truth this is an illegitimate comparison, then and now, because the technologies in which the two empires grew were so utterly different that they defied any validity in comparing the realities of the impact of their cultures upon other, less complex, technologies. One must begin, to be sure, with elements, societies, problems which are in truth comparable. What better, then, as any number of scholars have come to argue, than to compare frontiers, bound by the rubric of open space theory (or, as Hartz would have it, of fragment society analysis) as they are?

One other very real danger arises. Frontier theory is metaphor and myth as well as reality; the fact that Turner acknowledged the frontier to be a state of mind, and the manner of the examination of America's self-image in the work of Henry Nash Smith and Richard Slotkin,[26] confirm this. The problem is that frontier metaphors have a way of taking on a life of their own, not only in shoot-outs at the O.K. Corral and in bush ballads but also in political rhetoric and social purpose.[27] An example arises from South Africa.[28] In that nation the frontier metaphor fit historiographical needs happily for not one but three schools of thought, and as a result, examinations of the role of the frontier in South African history have fed not only the imperial school (as Mackinder did) and the antiimperial school (that is, in this instance, the Cape Liberal body of scholars), but the Afrikaner school as well. The last have seen the great trek as a myth of re-creation, just as Americans saw the West as a land of beginning again. The Cape Liberals, in turn, used the notion of the frontier to explain how wrong the Afrikaners were to have trekked away from modern civilization. Not only did the Enlightenment not follow into the interior of southern Africa; regression occurred. Until recently the use of frontier metaphor in South Africa thus made legitimate the total neglect of the history of the non-European peoples.[29]

The historian's tendency to use metaphor makes the words he writes far more literate than the words of the social scientists. But the historian tends to forget that the leap of faith between evidence and conclusion is substantially greater when one leaps not from the ice floes of fact to fact but from the ice pans of metaphor to metaphor. One highly literate and readable sociologist, Robert Nisbet, has written that a historical metaphor "is the synthesis of several complex units into one commanding image, . . . the expression of a complex idea not by analysis nor by direct statement but by sudden perception of analytical relation."[30] Or, as the geographer J. Wreford Watson has put it, geography induced through an analysis of images provides us with an understanding of the myths, not the facts, of the American scene.[31] The mental geography of regions conjured up by the use of frontier metaphors may serve many purposes: some liberating—as when Australians employed their frontier to put distance between themselves and the empire of which they were a part—and some merely stultifying, conservative, racist even.

To say that the frontier has been used in Australia in ways analogous to its use in South Africa is not to engage in a comparative analysis; rather, it is to say that in recent years the ghost at the table has been Louis Hartz, whose ideas require examination here if we are to understand how Australians use and view frontier theory. In

The Founding of New Societies Hartz extends the general argument
developed in his earlier work, *The Liberal Tradition in America*,[32]
in which he first put forward his idea of the "fragment society." In
that work he maintained that a centrist, liberal orthodoxy developed in America because its society was derived from the Enlightenment at a moment when it was possible to discard the constraints
of feudalism; that is, America did not have to fight to be free, it was
born free, and the American Revolution was the proof rather than
the cause of this condition. In something of an aside, Hartz suggested that the Chartist concept "had some effect in the settlement
of Australia"—an understatement—and had helped free Australia
from the "old European order."[33] In this assertion Hartz was following in the footsteps of Turner and Webb, in that almost by intuition
he grasped a truth which could be *made* demonstrable, accepting
as a given the difference between the old and the new. Hartz had
in mind a methodological concern: he was worried that historians
(he being in the Department of Government at Harvard) rejected
single-factor analyses out of hand on the ground that all historical
events were too complex to be attributed to a single cause. He was
right that historians do so, and for the reason he gave, but it was
not his intention to accept a single-factor analysis either; rather, he
wanted to remind historians, as he said, that "we must not . . .
brand as fruitless any attempt to isolate a significant historical variable and to study it by consistently comparing cases." For scientific
analysis required comparing cases. He wanted, then, to compare
those "new societies" which developed out of "frontier settings."
Later he would develop his argument in the introductory essay to
The Founding of New Societies.[34]

Hartz's analysis grew out of the continuum in which Turner and
Webb were situated. His method was similar, his clear joy with
what Allan Martin calls his "leaping vision" was infectious, and his
prophetic intent was clear.[35] Consider those scholars who have sought
to characterize the warp and woof of the American experience: Turner; Webb; David Potter, in his *People of Plenty*; C. Vann Woodward, in his essay "The Age of Reinterpretation"; Hartz himself.
Each pointed to not a single-, but a predominant-factor analysis:
Turner to the frontier, Webb to that same frontier enlarged and in
a new context, Potter to the idea of a natural economic abundance,

Woodward to the concept of a free security, and Hartz to the freedom of the fragment. Each was following a dialectic that derived from Hegel though at times it was similar to the dialectic of Marx (although with a vastly different end in view). Thesis clashed with antithesis, synthesis emerged, and, in time, under the impact of new experiences in a new environment, that synthesis became a thesis, again to be opposed by other new experiences, another antithesis, and in time another synthesis. The process was continued, Turner thought, until the triumph of that unique American type, Western man.

Behind the analysis one could see the desire to explicate inner truths, not only to demonstrate the uniqueness but in that uniqueness the superiority of America. Yet each of these prophets—for ultimately they were read as such, whatever their intentions—was at base pessimistic. Each felt the dynamic that had produced a unique America was no longer at work: The frontier had closed, Turner said. Four hundred years of boom were over, according to Webb. Natural economic abundance no longer was available to Americans, Potter concluded. No longer could Americans enjoy a security either free of cost or free of moral compromise, Woodward suggested. The fragments no longer were a fragment of a parent culture; they were mature and likely to sink into the sins of that maturity, Hartz warned. All were "catastrophic historians" who anticipated great change, most likely not for the better. Each fragment, Hartz concluded, would confront major crises as its own frontier closed. This was comparative history with a vengeance visited upon all, history that could admit to the uniqueness of the Australian frontier while linking it not only to a type but also to a process in common.

This is not the place to examine how it is that Hartz went wrong. For he did go wrong, in that his theory, except at the highest level of generalization, does not survive the Australian facts. Rather, my recitation of the evolution in comparative history from Turner to Hartz is to make my second long-delayed point of relevance: that Americans, at least, have ever been eager to read the history of other nations in terms of the history of their own, precisely as Webb showed. And Americans have shown a paradoxical desire to prove that their history has been an exception to the Old World while making their history the normative experience, the departure point, for other histories in other societies based upon white settlement. Allan Nevins was prescient when, just after World War II, he went to Australia and wrote of the United States as the Old World.[36] Our historians sought to fix upon Australia, New Zealand, and to a lesser extent South Africa, the formulaic devices of a historiography developed initially to liberate the American experience; Turner and Webb were America's Pirenne and Michelet, bringing a cake of custom to the South Pacific even as they broke that cake when looking eastward across the Atlantic. That Australian scholars should have first found Turner attractive, as Adams and others found the Teutonic forest attractive, should surprise us no more than that subsequent generations of Australian scholars should reject Turner and the continuum.

Others have provided a full critique of Hartz; others have written in detail of what Australian scholars said about their frontier after reading Turner and Webb.[37] I refer all who would seek a superb bibliography of the many articles and few books devoted to this subject, together with a careful look at the content of those writings, to an earlier volume in the Walter Prescott Webb Memorial Lectures.[38] I seek here to take up ground somewhat different from that already occupied. My first purpose has been to suggest not why Australians were fascinated with frontier theory but why Americans were eager that they should be so.

But I do not intend solely an exercise in intellectual history. To stop here without discussing the frontier itself would be to leave the stage before the Prince of Denmark had appeared. I turn back, therefore, to Russel Ward and his work, *The Australian Legend.*

As the title of his 1958 book should have made clear, Ward was primarily interested in examining a legend, in looking at what a people had come to believe was true of their past and, by implication, their present. To do this he had to examine the facts as usually understood, in order to see which portions of the self-vision partook of legend and which did not, and he also had to see how those portions and the proportions between them changed. His book was a complex mixture of fact and fancy; he almost always was structurally clear as to which was which. It was a major and hideously complex undertaking, and as one might expect, on occasion the distinction between legend and fact was not clear enough to satisfy

everyone. Several readers flatly misunderstood the book. One re-
viewer, a critic fully capable of subtle insights of his own, suggested
that Ward was confused: "While our national mythology is totally
coloured by rural experience, the fact is that Australia is one of the
most highly urbanized countries on earth."[39] This critic argued that
since it was demonstrable that most Australians were and always
had been city-dwellers, the outback could not have had the influence Ward attributed to it. Clearly this critic had not read (or had
rejected) his Henry Nash Smith, for Ward's point was that whatever
the facts might be in terms of demography, it was patently clear
that most Australians believed something different of themselves.
Here again a historian was being hoist for choosing to write about
what a people believed to be true rather than about the so-called
objective truth.

To be sure, Ward was playing a dangerous game. As James C.
Malin remarked long ago, to write intellectual history is to try to
nail jelly to the wall.[40] Ward was doing much as Turner had done in
asserting a truth and then seeking to account for it. Obviously he
could not examine all evidence of how Australians perceived themselves; all intellectual history is open to the charge of being improp-
erly selective, of looking for patterns rather than to the linear pro-
gression we call chronology. Obviously, too, such history can fall off
into that dangerous area where it is possible for the wily to slip any
noose by declaring that whatever is imputed to them, indeed whatever they said, was not "precisely what was meant." But Ward had
no intention of being wily; he was interested in a gritty question
which related to the history of the Australian *people* rather than to
an elite group. As he wrote in 1978 in "The Australian Legend Re-
visited," in a retrospective issue of *Historical Studies* devoted to his
work, his book was not meant to be a balanced history of Australia;
it was "an attempt 'to trace and explain the development of [the]
national *mystique.*'"[41] He looked to the bush: "Poets, painters and
drinkers in public houses recognise Ned Kelly, or Ben Hall, or the
'Man from Snowy River' . . . as embodiments of Australian characteristics." Of course Ward knew what he was doing in the way Henry
Nash Smith knew what he did: they were scholars who, while writing scholarly works, were engaged in the Great Game, contributing
to the very way contemporary society felt about itself and, by ex-

tension, how that society would attempt to meet the future. In this sense historians like Turner, Webb, Woodward, and Ward were far more important to the *national* security than dozens of senators at work on dozens of investigatory subcommittees.

Let us look in brief compass at the Australian frontier itself. To show Ward's method, which I admire, I will summarize my own view of the Australian frontier, indicating where he and I most clearly disagree. Of necessity I crib the next several paragraphs from that which I have written before.[42]

There have been at least four clearly distinguishable Australian "frontiers." Further, Australia (like the United States and together with New Zealand) was itself viewed as a frontier of European civilization from the end of the eighteenth century until the latter decades of the nineteenth. This is not alone because *Terra Australis Incognita*, the great unknown land of the south, so haunted European (and especially British and French) imaginations. Fundamental to the development of Australia, and of its frontiers, is the fact that the Australian population was until World War II 95 percent or more British in stock. Unlike the frontiers of North America, where highly diverse European peoples came together to rub customs off on one another, Australia has represented a transplantation, virtually complete and only with those changes induced by the environment, of British lower and lower middle class culture. Australia therefore was a *British* frontier, a land of beginning again for a variety of peoples who had been unsuccessful, or who were unhappy, in Britain: convicts, remittance men, Chartists, Irish who opposed the church and the rule of the United Kingdom, and dissident religious groups—Methodists foremost. To the Australia of the First Fleet were transplanted many of the religious and class quarrels of nineteenth-century Britain.

Internally, the four or more frontiers at first were relatively distinct. The first lay around Sydney Cove, where in January, 1788, the First Fleet of eleven storeships and transports, under the command of Arthur Phillip, disgorged its contents together with over a thousand convicts and jailers. About lay the Bush, and within the Bush lay aborigines whose Stone Age culture ill prepared them to deal with the newcomers. Convicts were sent to New South Wales until 1840 and to Tasmania until 1852; in all, some 160,000 arrived, primarily after 1815 (Western Australia also received convicts from 1850 to 1868). Convict settlements were the antithesis of those in northern North America: the men were tied to a system, itself ill-organized and inefficient, which precluded free land, social innovation, and the breaking of class barriers through individual performance. In time the majority of convicts were assigned to free settlers, providing a labor force, intensifying class awareness, rooting settlement near the ports of entry, Sydney and Hobart, and retarding the growth of forms of agriculture which were not amenable to a gang-labor system. If there were a true frontier at this time, it lay beyond these settlements in the Bush, which—precisely because it was at the outer edge of imprisonment—became increasingly attractive, romantic, and remote.

The Bush was not, in fact, attractive at all, being exceptionally inhospitable to settlement. Australian ground cover was prickly, poor, and weakly rooted; the land was arid, water evaporated quickly, and the timber cover was sparse except in relatively limited areas, such as the Blue Mountains. Compact settlements were difficult to establish—even as the convict period ended—for lack of water and the poverty of transport kept most Australians bound to the seacoast, as they remain to this day. The obvious solution to the near interior was a pastoral economy, and a second frontier emerged upon the basis of sheep.

This second frontier was that of the squatter. Climate and soil did not favor small settlers, and the grants made to emancipists and garrison men were too small to permit wheat farming. Small settlers lacked capital for expansion, limiting most free settlers to market gardening near small towns. The New South Wales Corps enjoyed near monopolistic advantages, especially over the importation of rum, and after John Macarthur built a fortune on rum, he applied his knowledge of monopoly to wool. The economy that arose was not a democratic one, resting as it did upon men of capital, and a pastoral economy developed rapidly. From 1821, the first year for commercial export of wool, to 1850, Australian wool growers moved from experimenters upon the fringes of an empire to the proven producers of the greatest amount of wool for England, despite the immense distances, surpassing Germany and Spain together. Middle-class immigrants were now more attracted to Australia; many had been comfortable in Britain but faced the prospect of a decline, and they took with them sufficient capital to establish a squatocracy upon the land, ultimately becoming a local equivalent of the gentry-bred squireocracy of England.

In the second quarter of the nineteenth century, pastoral settlement spread over the potential inland grazing area of south-eastern Australia, and in 1836 the government recognized this diffusion by imposing an annual license on squatters who had entered the officially "unsettled" districts. This licensing asserted the Crown's title to the lands. Three years later the unsettled lands were divided into nine squatting districts, a border police system was established, and a commissioner of Crown lands was named for each district. In 1847 the permanency of the squatters was recognized when New South Wales (which included Victoria and Queensland) was divided into settled, intermediate, and unsettled districts, with one-, eight-, and fourteen-year leases allowed to squatters. The society that developed bore little relationship to the frontier communities of North America; there was little fear of a native population (driven to extinction in Tasmania and forced into the dead heart of the mainland). The frontier of the squatter bore more resemblances to that of the *trekboer* in South Africa.

During this period exploration of the interior of Australia began to confirm the initial impression: climate would not permit the settlers a wide range of choice in economic activities. Few rivers offered access to the inland; many of the lakes went utterly dry during the summer; valleys ended in blind canyons below high plateaus. Early movement, therefore, was along the coastal lowlands. In 1813, however, the Blue Mountains were penetrated deeply enough to reveal open woodland to the west, and the first inland town, Bathurst, was founded two years later. Within eight years there were sheep stations at Limestone Plains. In 1837 Sir Thomas Mitchell, the surveyor-general, traveled from Sydney to Portland Bay (in western Victoria), opening a rich pastoral area which he named Australia Felix. Most important, Charles Sturt sought to find some Australian equivalent of the North American Great Lakes by following the westward-draining rivers from the eastern highlands, only to prove that nothing lay in the interior except more salt pans. Further to the north a German, Ludwig Leichhardt, crossed the continent to a point north of Darwin, discovering that, once away from the tropical lowlands, the north was as arid as the south. In 1848 Leichhardt disappeared while attempting another transcontinental journey, and he, above all, became the symbol of the unpromising, omnivorous Outback, the land not of beginning again or of the eternal return but of never return. Upon Leichhardt would be built many of the legends of the Australian "frontiers," as well as the finest work of the continent's finest author, Patrick White, in *Voss*.

Settlement of Australia, its exploration, and, to the degree that such took place, its interior development, proceeded from the east and south. The far west was isolated by the great distances of the interior. Communication continued to be by sea, and Australians continued to cluster in seaport villages. Railways were built by the colonial governments, since private enterprise could not expect profit from intermediate communities of settlers, and the Australian grain farmer, in particular, demanded cheaper transportation to the ports. Victoria had more capital and began railway development by the late 1850s, but its railways did not reach the South Australian border until 1885—less than a quarter of the way across the continent—the same year that the first trans-Canadian railway was completed. To this day Australian distances decree travel by air.

Another frontier lay, therefore, to the east of Perth, and it rested on sheep, on minerals, and on timber. (In 1883 one of the richest silver-lead-zinc fields in the world was found at Broken Hill, in New South Wales, and from it, from Tasmania, and then from Western Australia would come much new capital.) Westralia remained an economic appendage of the east, just as Queensland—where sugarcane began to the grown commercially from the 1850s—was dependent on its southeast, and the dryland farmers of South Australia were dependent on Victoria and New South Wales. Instead of creating new cultural centers—as the gold rushes and mining boom of Canada and the United States had provided to British Columbia, California, and the Rocky Mountains—mining in Australia sharpened the focus of the continent on its two rapidly growing cities, Melbourne and Sydney.

A fourth frontier for Australia lay not within the continent but outside: to the far north, in New Guinea. Populated with Stone Age cultures which European imperialism had passed by until the 1870s,

New Guinea was at first of interest only because it attracted the attention of Germany and because it could provide some *kanaka* labor for the Queensland cane fields. Australia's West Africa, it was regarded as too tropical for white settlement, its unattractive aspect reflecting that it was "the land God had made on a Saturday night." Queensland asserted its presence there in 1884, largely for reasons of security; Britain transferred Papua to Australia in 1902; and in 1914 Australian troops took over the German portion of the island. This land was confirmed to the Commonwealth of Australia—itself the new birth of 1901—by the League of Nations in 1919. There was no immediate rush of settlers, however.[43]

In terms of open space, much of Australia remains unsettled today, and in this sense frequently it is referred to as one of the world's last frontiers. But if by "frontier" is meant something more subtle than the mere absence of people, Australia is not and never was a true frontier. In particular, relatively little of the classic formulation of a Turnerian frontier applies to the Australian story. Consider the differences.

The Australian interior proved to be desert; Australia was not a land of abundance in terms of variety, and it did not offer a range of entrepreneurial opportunities, encouraging concentration of land and monopolistic trading practices rather than free enterprise on the North American model. From the first moment of settlement the average Australian lived in a small town; today two-thirds of the population lives in six cities, all on or near the coast. As Sir Keith Hancock has remarked in his autobiography, Australians had "trams on the mind": those who lived in the small towns behind the Blue Mountains, the Dandenongs, or the low hills around the ports hankered not for movement further west, not for distance between themselves and others, but for closeness, compactness, and a homogeneous society. *Mateship*, the characteristic Australian term for comradeship, grew in an ambivalent manner from a fear of the Outback as well as from romantic involvement with it, for the Outback required a mate instead of promoting individualism. Australia was an urban society, and Australian democracy sprang not from its frontier but from its asphalted cities. To be sure, Jack was as good as his master, but the source of this demand lay in the Chartism of industrial workers, in English lower-class radicalism transplanted almost whole and kept intact in an alien environment. To be sure, Australians were transformed by their environment, but the fact that environment dictates the outer limits of opportunity is not particularly Turnerian as a conception, as the first Biblical wanderers in the wilderness knew. Australians did not embrace nature and did not assume that one must get back to the land to stand erect. They did not approve of mixing peoples, and they did not emphasize individualism.

To be sure, there were similarities to the Turnerian model as well, of course, and unsurprisingly so, since this model was highly elastic and capable of embracing contradictions. Australians showed a sense of destiny not unlike that of the first settlers to press beyond the Missouri. They were a violent people, given to quick solutions to immediate problems. They admired the new—but held to the old. They moved often from place to place, showing a North American physical and social mobility—but the place-to-place movement generally was from town to town, city to city. Perhaps most important, Australians did embrace a *myth* of the frontier, of the Outback, just as Canadians and Americans embraced myths of their own. Australian literature is filled with the balladry, the poetry, and the plain voices of "a harsh land, a land that swings, like heart and blood, from heat to mist" (Ian Mudie). Ned Kelly, a Wild Colonial Boy, and other bushrangers would become the plain man's cultural heroes, not alone for being independent but also for being men who opposed a system which was urban, capitalistic, and imperially oriented. Australia's most famous painter, Sidney Nolan, who painted Kelly over and over, had caught exactly the Australian frontier and the Australian difference: alone, alienated, distant, and yet fascinated with a mechanical civilization in which however far across the horizon train tracks might run, they inevitably ended at a port, beyond which stood the world upon which Australia depended, a world that could dash Australian hopes.

So much for the summary. While mine, it is not particularly original; indeed, as Russel Ward remarked upon being exposed to it, I appear to be in parallel to most of the scholars on the subject except for himself and, to a lesser extent, H. C. Allen in his book *Bush and Backwoods*.[44] Ward feels that we are in substantial disagreement, as he finds himself in disagreement with most Australian scholars, for he believes the Australian frontier to have had much that was Turnerian in it and correctly feels that I do not. We have six points of significant difference, he argues.[45]

My reason for summarizing these six differences in point of view is not to engage in tedious debate over matters of detail, for I have a larger issue in mind. But first, the areas of disagreement: Ward notes that I believe the first frontier was bush around Sydney and feels that this implies subsequent frontiers were not bush as well, when certainly the pastoral or sheep frontier was such. Second, he notes that later research made it clear that many early squatters did not bring capital from Britain but were currency lads, poor immigrants, and even old convict hands. Third, he feels it "blindingly wrong" to assert that the Australian frontier was not Turnerian, since occupation and development proceeded from the eastern coast westward and, later, from the southeastern coast westward and northward, just as in the United States. He also points out that California developed separately, in relative isolation, as Western Australia did. Fourth, he argues that the gold rushes caused growth of inland towns at a rate even faster than the growth of Melbourne and Sydney. Fifth, he finds the notion of New Guinea as an Australian frontier "a bizarre idea equivalent to naming the Philippines, Hawaii or Alaska" an American frontier. Finally, his pungent comment on my belief that mateship reflected a fear of the Outback is that "words fail" him, and he finds my reference to Nolan quite contradictory of that conclusion.

I will not concede any of these points to Professor Ward, except to acknowledge that on two of them I wrote badly and thus obscurely. That California and Western Australia both developed in isolation strikes me as having little to do with Turner; rather, that California was an appendage of the East relates more to present-day dependency theory than to Turnerian open space theory.[46] That the gold rushes brought many people into inland towns in the second half of the nineteenth century does not seem to me to vitiate the fact that two great cities continued to dominate services, access to the world, and development to a far greater extent than New York, Boston, and Philadelphia dominated the Colorado, Montana, or Nevada mining towns. That Hawaii and Alaska were part of an expanding American empire (as defined by Webb) seems patently true, and was precisely my point, and that the empire not only was created when the frontier was closed but also was seen to be closed within the continental United States also seems clearly true.[47] Finally, I see no contradiction between romantic involvement and fear; indeed, as I read psychosexuality, this seems a commonplace.[48]

My point by now is obvious. One scholar writes of Australia as an Australian. He wishes to free it from being seen in the context of imperial history. Perhaps he sees Turnerian parallels as one means of doing so. Certainly he places Australian meanings upon what he sees, and quite appropriately so. Another scholar's perceptions arise out of the American experience, and he comes to his views of Australia less from Turner than from Ronald Robinson and Jack Gallagher,[49] less from class analysis and more from use of the collaborator model as constructed by imperial historians, less from an interest in what the Australian experience says about Australia and more from what it does in helping us to test the body of thought usually subsumed as dependency theory. Asking different questions produces different answers. Neither set is necessarily wrong.

A larger point emerges. The frontier is an excellent perspective on Australia. But it is only one perspective. Comparative studies "illuminate historical discussion after the manner of an imaginative and disciplined use of simile, metaphor and analogy."[50] The words are C. Vann Woodward's. When Louis Hartz used Australia to throw light on American history, he was studying Australia for the reason Americans might most reasonably be expected to study it—that is, for reasons of their own. He studied Australia for the reasons Webb wanted Europeans to study America. Hartz's purpose was to comment on America; had his purpose been another, for example to promote theoretical ends relating to the methodology of comparative studies, he would have needed to do far more.[51] If one wishes to isolate for consideration the role of the frontier in a variety of societies, one must study those societies entirely before the act of isolation may be attempted; frontier history must be the end in view, not the beginning and not the means.

To understand Australia one must, to be sure, see it in terms of frontier analogies. But one must do far more. Questions relating to the nature of governance, the transfer and diffusion of cultural norms, the establishment of prefabricated collaborators in a settler community, even the nature and actions of the men on the spot—history as the essence of innumerable biographies—must all be taken into consideration. Ward does this, as Hartz did it, from an oblique angle. Ultimately each, being interested in what a people believed to be true of themselves, has created the self-fulfilling prophecy in which that which is believed to be true becomes a kind of truth.

It is, in part, this problem with which Geoffrey Blainey has dealt in his book *The Tyranny of Distance*, first published in 1966.[52] The argument of the book can be quickly summarized. He explicitly places the idea of distance in the stead of Turner's frontier thesis.[53] Australia must, Blainey argues, be viewed less as a continent than as a series of islands—of coastal cities which until recently communicated with one another best by sea and which were surrounded by water and inhospitable or largely unsettled land. Distance determined Australia's history in the way Ross Calvin said that the sky determined New Mexico's.[54] Australia was shaped by distance, as the frontier buffered America: distance from people, from markets, from the protection of the Mother Country. This distance made Australians self-reliant; the internal distances to be conquered made them aggressive; low population density and lack of cheap labor assured that the state would build the railways which in the United States were built by private enterprise. Sea strategy dictated the sites of the early outposts. Wool and gold were feasible exports because their value was high in relation to freight costs. Voluntary, self-subsidized migration from Europe was rarer than in North America because of the distance; migration had to be state-maintained. Despite a rugged outback and an apparent frontier, the people became state-oriented, dependent from the outset on the city. A mixed-enterprise economy emerged. The scarcity of Australian workmen meant that they could exert maximum political influence and move the nation quickly toward social welfare, while a steady stream of working-class immigrants to the United States acted against the idea of welfare. In the latter, *welfarism* became a pejorative term; in Australia it was generally judged to be "a good thing."[55]

The frontier was measured less in terms of the nature of groups moving onto the land than in terms of technological changes relating to the sea: clipper ships, steamships, telegraphy, motorized ships, refrigerated cargo vessels, airplanes. World War I taught Australia that it was close enough to Europe (and its problems) to supply men but too far away to supply primary produce, and as the ratio of time needed to reach Europe compared to that need to get to Asia diminished, Australians began to rethink their position in world affairs. Ultimately Australians found that distance forced Britain to desert them, and many willingly accepted the protection of the United States. The art of loneliness and exile, the novels of Patrick White and the poetry of A. D. Hope, the paintings of Sidney Nolan, reflected this acute awareness that distance placed Australia at the hither edge of a contracting frontier, of a Europe less and less able to be a major presence in the Australian future. The ties to Britain weakened, and a spirit of separateness grew in the land. As Blainey concluded, "Much of Australia's history had been shaped by the contradiction that it depended intimately and comprehensively on a country which was farther away than almost any other in the world."[56]

Even in so superficial a summary, the points of departure from Turner, Webb, and Ward may be seen. Equally well, one may see that Blainey is part of the continuum: his is an extension of the frontier thesis while also drawing upon dependency theory. Again the dialectical method is apparent, with technological innovation substituted for cultural transformation; again the tone is prophetic, the writing leans heavily on metaphor, and the manner and mood of Turner and Webb are much in evidence. Blainey's last sentence is no less elegiac, nervous, and catastrophic than the conclusions of Turner, Potter, and Woodward: "The Antipodes were drifting, though where they were drifting no one knew."[57]

One group of Australians did not find Europeans so distant, of course. This was the indigenous Australian population, now called the central Australian aborigine. Most frontier historiographies have, until recently, omitted the native peoples except as backdrops to highlight the technology and skills of the settler groups. In the whole of Turner's *The Frontier in American History* there are nine references to Indians; there are also nine references to capital and sixteen to individualism.[58] While the aborigine plays a greater role in Ward's work, it is a small role nonetheless. Webb makes relatively few references to American Indians, although he notes in particular the function of the "noble savage" in literature in a fine and over-looked chapter.[59]

Each of us contributing to this volume has been asked to consider four common themes: the persistence and change of institutions and attitudes on the frontier; the role of government in promoting and controlling frontier advancement and development; the treatment of native populations; and the environmental impact of the frontier movement. I have focused openly elsewhere on one of these themes—that of the treatment of native populations[60]—while attempting to say quite a bit here about the first two themes. The fourth I have neglected, save in one sense. In examining the historiographical environment in which the debate about the relevance of Turner and Webb had taken place, I have sought to suggest something about environment, in the broadest sense of the word, and something more about impact. Yet, as I have suggested, impact studies do not strike me as comparative studies. If a comparison is to be made, it must be made by those who read the four discrete, separate presentations on Brazil, Canada, Australia, and South Africa.[61]

Above all, more than meeting a commitment to coherence, more than looking again at Turner or Webb or even Australia, I have wanted to strike another note. If I have been critical of the metaphorical, of the proud and the emotional, in Turner and Webb, it is because I wish to be self-critical; I do not mean to leave the impression that I dislike their kind of history. Rather, I admire it. I much prefer the leap of faith, the daredevil act of Walter Prescott Webb as he moved from ice floe to ice floe, to the labor of a historian whose regard is above all for setting fact upon fact in precise sequence—although such work, too, must count. The excitement, the fun, the significance of history arises from precisely what Webb declared it to be in his presidential address to the American Historical Association—History as High Adventure.[62]

NOTES

1. Boston, 1952.
2. Webb, *Great Frontier*, p. 7.

3. *The Old World and the New, 1492–1650* (Cambridge: Cambridge University Press, 1970), p. 57.

4. Webb, *Great Frontier*, p. 182.

5. Ibid., p. 190.

6. Mary Durack, *Kings in Grass Castles* (London: Constable, 1959), p. 3.

7. Webb, *Great Frontier*, pp. 6, 411.

8. For an elaboration of this argument, see Robin W. Winks, ed., *Other Voices, Other Views* (Westport, Conn.: Greenwood, 1978), pp. 6–9. Interestingly, the Denver newspapers took great offense at Webb's analysis, for by calling Colorado a desert, he was not a "booster."

9. Melbourne, 1958.

10. Cambridge, Mass.: Harvard University Press, 1950.

11. See Kenneth A. MacKirdy, "Australia," in *The Historiography of the British Empire-Commonwealth*, ed. Robin W. Winks (Durham, N.C.: Duke University Press, 1966), pp. 137–73.

12. See, among many books, John Mayston Bechervaise, *Australia: World of Difference* (London: Angus & Robertson, 1967).

13. New York, 1964.

14. See Bernard Semmel, *Imperialism and Social Reform* (Cambridge, Mass.: Harvard University Press, 1960), pp. 166–76; Robert B. Downs, *Books That Changed the World* (New York: Mentor Books, 1956), pp. 107–17, and Anthony J. Pearce, introduction to reprint edition of Sir Halford John Mackinder, *Democratic Ideals and Reality* (New York: Norton, 1962), pp. ix–xxiv.

15. The reference is to New Zealand, of course. The quotation is used in Downs, *Books That Changed the World*, p. 109.

16. Mackinder "Geographical Pivot of History," *Geographical Journal*, 23 (Apr., 1904): 421.

17. Elliott, *Old World and New*, pp. 59 ff.

18. Alexander, *Moving Frontiers: An American Theme and Its Application in Australian History* (Melbourne: Melbourne University Press, 1947).

19. Harper, "The Rural and Urban Frontiers," *Australian Journal of Science*, 25 (Feb., 1963): 321–34.

20. See especially Brian W. Blouet, *Sir Halford Mackinder, 1861–1947: Some New Perspectives*, University of Oxford School of Geography Research Paper 13 (Oxford, 1975).

21. *Geographical Journal*, 23 (1904): 441.

22. "Australians and the Comparative Frontier," *Essays on Walter Prescott Webb* (Austin: University of Texas Press, 1976), pp. 17–52, and "A Brief Message for the Young and/or Ambitious: Comparative Frontiers as a Field for Investigation," *Western Historical Quarterly*, 9 (Jan., 1978): 5–18.

23. Mikesell is particularly inclusive: "Comparative Studies in Frontier History," *Annals of the Association of American Geographers*, 50 (Mar., 1960): 62–74.

24. Webb, like Turner, was roundly attacked by Fred Shannon, and Webb's defense (and occasional lack of it) is particularly revealing. See Shannon, *Critiques of Research in the Social Sciences: An Appraisal of Walter Prescott Webb's The Great Plains, A Study in Institutions and Environment* (New York, 1940), and Webb's article, "Geographical-Historical Concepts in American History," *Annals of the Association of American Geographers*, 50 (June, 1960): 83–93, with a commentary by D. W. Meining.

25. The following three paragraphs are paraphrased from my *The Relevance of Canadian History* (Toronto: Macmillan, 1979), pp. xii–xiii, 1.

26. *Regeneration through Violence: The Mythology of the American Frontier, 1600–1860* (Middletown, Conn.: Wesleyan University Press, 1973).

27. See Russel Ward, ed., *The Penguin Book of Australian Ballads* (Harmondsworth: Penguin, 1964), pp. 118–36.

28. I am grateful to Leonard Thompson for allowing me to attend certain sessions of his course Comparative Frontier History: South Africa and for the use of the bibliography accompanying that course, and to Gerald McSheffrey for pointing me to additional materials.

29. See Harrison M. Wright, *The Burden of the Present: Liberal-Radical Controversy over Southern African History* (Cape Town: David Philip, 1977).

30. *Social Change in History* (New York: Knopf, 1969), p. 4.

31. "Image Geography: The Myth of America in the American Scene," *Advancement of Science*, no. 27 (1970–71):1–9.

32. *The Founding of New Societies* (New York: Harcourt, Brace, 1955).

33. Ibid., pp. 20–21.

34. The best examination of Hartz on Australia is Allen Martin's "Australia and the Hartz 'Fragment' Thesis," paper read to the Conference on British Studies, New York, 1967.

35. Ibid., p. 5.

36. Nevins, *Old America in a Young World* (New York: Newcomen Society, 1945).

37. Jackson, "A Brief Message," *Western Historical Quarterly*, 9 (Jan., 1978): 5–18.

38. Several articles of relevance which escaped Jackson's net have appeared recently in *Historical Studies: Australia and New Zealand*.

39. Max Harris, "Morals and Manners," in *Australia Civilization: A Symposium*, ed. Peter Coleman (Melbourne: F. W. Cheshire, 1962), p. 50.

40. It is especially in intellectual history, of course, that problems of definition arise.

41. *Historical Studies: Australia and New Zealand*, 18 (Oct., 1978): 171.

42. The twelve paragraphs that follow (although revised) are drawn from my essay in Howard R. Lamar, ed., *The Reader's Encyclopedia of the American West* (New York: Corwell, 1977), pp. 415–16.

43. See Donald G. Gordon, *The Australian Frontier in New Guinea, 1870–1885* (New York: Columbia University Press, 1959).

44. Subtitled *A Comparison of the Frontier in Australia and the United States* (East Lansing: Michigan State University Press, 1959).

45. Correspondence between Russel Ward and myself, 1978.

46. See especially Joseph A. Kahl, *Modernization, Exploitation and Dependency in Latin America: Germani, Gonzalez Casanova and Cordoso* (New Brunswick, N.J.: Transaction Books, 1976).

47. I am now at work on a book. "The Idea of American Imperialism." As an approach to it, see my *Relevance of Canadian History*, pp. 60–86.

48. Michel Foucault, *Historie de la sexualite*, I (Paris: Librarie Plon, 1976).

49. See William Roger Louis, ed., *Imperialism: The Robinson and Gallagher Controversy* (New York: Franklin Watts, 1976).

50. C. Vann Woodward, ed., *The Comparative Approach to American History* (New York: Basic Books, 1968).

51. For one statement on this problem, see Stanley Seaberg, *Teaching the Comparative Approach to American Studies* (New York: Council on Education, 1971).

52. Melbourne, 1966.

53. Blainey, *Tyranny*, p. ix.

54. Calvin, *Sky Determines*, rev. ed. (Albuquerque: University of New Mexico Press, 1965).

55. See Geoffrey Blainey and Donald Horne, *The Lucky Country: Australia Today* (Baltimore: Penguin, 1964).

56. Blainey, *Tyranny*, p. 339.

57. Ibid.

58. New York, 1920.

59. Webb, *Great Frontier*, p. 364.

60. At this point in the delivery of the lecture I paused to analyze in some detail the comparative nature of race relations in Australia and New Zealand, posing four factors in particular that accounted for the differences: the nature of the white settler groups, the nature of the indigenous population, the nature of the landscape over which the conflict took place, and the nature and degree of commitment on the part of the metropolitan power. I omit those fourteen paragraphs from the published version here; the essence of them was stated briefly in my *The Myth of the American Frontier: Its Relevance to America, Canada and Australia* (Leicester: Leicester University Press, 1971).

61. I attended the other three Walter Prescott Webb lectures for 1979, and the other speakers attended mine. In all of our talks we engaged in a variety of asides meant to resonate off one of the other speakers' subjects; these asides are omitted here.

62. I should like to make mention here of a valuable essay that appeared (despite its date) after I presented the present paper: G. M. Tobin, "Landscape, Region, and the Writing of History: Walter Prescott Webb in the 1920s," *American Studies International*, 16 (Summer, 1978): 7–18. Mr. Tobin is an Australian. For "History as High Adventure," see Webb's collection of essays, *An Honest Preface and Other Essays* (Boston: Houghton Mifflin, 1959).

DATE DUE

JAN 0 8 2001			
GAYLORD			PRINTED IN U.S.A.